No Passion
Or Too Many
Passions
To **Focus** On?

The Secrets To Find Your Passion And
Life Purpose, Find The One Passion That
You Meant To Work On Your Lifetime

Dr. Beau Young

Copyright © 2020 Dr. Beau Young.

All rights reserved. No part of this book may be reproduced, stored, or transmitted by any means—whether auditory, graphic, mechanical, or electronic—without written permission of both publisher and author, except in the case of brief excerpts used in critical articles and reviews. Unauthorized reproduction of any part of this work is illegal and is punishable by law.

Interior design by FormattedBooks

Contents

Introduction ix

Chapter 1: Where Are You Now? Find Yourself Through Self-Diagnostic Tools! 1

Why Am I Unhappy Right Now? 2
Why Is It Important To Get In Touch With Yourself? 4
Self-diagnostics Through Checklists 6
Self-diagnostic Through Journaling 13
Self-diagnostic Through Projects: Creating A Dream Board To Visualize Your Wildest Ambitions 17
Self-diagnostic Through Personality Tests 18

Chapter 2: What You Don't Want: Setting Boundaries In Your Professional Life 19

Examine Your Whys To Figure Out Which Wants Aren't Really Wants At All 20
Get Rid Of The Shoulds That Don't Add Up With Your Wants 21
Exercises To Find Out What Wastes Your Time 23
How To Say No 26

Chapter 3: The Ultimate Guide To Facing Your Fears 29

Understanding Fear: What Is It? 30
What Does Fear Feel Like To You? 32
Changing Your Diet To Decrease Your Fear 33
Six Everyday Exercises To Face Fear 35
Everyday Strategies To Face Your Fears Your Fears 39

Chapter 4: How To Free Yourself From Distractions 43

The Three Biggest Distractions That Hold Us Back 44
Identify What's Holding You Back 48
How To Eliminate The Non-essential 49
Everyday Exercises To Build Focus 53

Chapter 5: Listen To Your Heart And Not Your Head 57

It's Scientifically Proven That You Should Do What You
Love And Not What You Think Is Logical! 58
Everyday Exercises To Start Listening To Your Heart 60
Strategies To Commit To Listening To Your Heart 63

Chapter 6: Define Your Passion In 10 Questions 65

What Passion Is And Isn't 67
The Questions 69

Chapter 7: Too Many Passions? Which Is Profitable? 75

What Is Fear Of Better Options (FOBO) And How To
Get Over It? 76
How Is FOBO Connected To Passion? 78
Narrow Down Your Passions Through Questions 78
Use The Internet To Narrow Down Your Passions 81

Still Got Too Many Passions? Try The 2-week Mini-
project Technique To Narrow Down Your Passions 83

Chapter 8: The Law Of Attraction: How To Use It to Conquer All Hurdles 87

The 7 Laws Of Attraction 89
Celebrities Who Have Used The Law Of Attraction 91
Ways To Use The Law Of Attraction Every Day 94

Chapter 9: Convert Your Passion Into A Profession 97

Differentiating Between A Hobby And A Profitable Passion ... 97
3 Steps To Getting Your Project Underway 101
Two Paths Through Which You Can Pursue Your Passion ... 103

Conclusion 107
Resources 111

Your Success Booklet
(Read this before you start any success journey...)

This booklet includes:

- ➢ 9 things that successful people are different from the mediocre
- ➢ 15 things successful people say no to
- ➢ 8 Steps to achieve anything you want in life

Get yourself mentally equipped before the journey starts.
To receive your success booklet, visit the link:

https://beausuccess.activehosted.com/f/1

Introduction

> "The only way to do great work is to love what you do.
> If you haven't found it yet, keep looking. Don't settle."
> —Steve Jobs

How did you feel when TED talks of successful entrepreneurs, experts on television, your childhood best friend, and college counselor all advise you the same thing?
Just follow your passion!

Yeah, sure, you'd love to—if only you knew what your passion was.

Did you know that according to a poll, 85% of workers worldwide admit hating their jobs? That's right, 85 percent! A number this high can't be a coincidence, right?

Then, you might ask who is discovering planets and galaxies? Who is making advancements in areas of robotics and artificial intelligence employing cutting edge technologies every step of the way? Who is creating music which resonates in our heads the whole day despite listening to it only once? Who are these people dominating the world and the skies above?

It is that underrepresented minority of 15 percent of people who listened to their hearts; put their souls in their work, invented, created, and innovated. Life wasn't always easy for successful people. They ran, hid, and jumped from place to place in the arena of the world until they finally managed to drape the red cloth and dominate the bull—their *one* true passion.

Are you living in a black hole?
Do you numb yourself with TV, the Internet, and video games?
If yes, you are not alone. Because the vast majority of people who feel fearful, out of control, and incapable of managing their increasingly demanding lives, do the same.

If you find yourself constantly lacking motivation, dread going to your job, find what you're doing dull, and repetitive, you have come to the right place. In the step-by-step guide, you will find what is working well for you in your current life & career. What do you find content, meaningful, and enjoyable? And how to reclaim your life and how to obliterate the hopelessness and despair that take hold and just won't go away.

Imagine a different world:
Every day you open your eyes, you can't wait to jump out of bed and get to work. You work extra longer and harder than everyone else, but it is not difficult for you because you enjoy it. You are often lost in that state of mind of *flow*, where you forget about time, completely immersed in your work. You are pulled forward by big goals, yet happy where you are now. Feeling the satisfaction of growth and cherishing your luck at the same time. Work is not exactly what many people think of it; it's not just an "occupation" or a "job" but a *passion, a life purpose*.

If your life is not like that, you might have missed something that is extremely important to you. And if you never make an effort to find what it is, such a thing will never be possible.

Here's an important question:
Can you find your passion in a car garage?

Most people would agree that such a thing is too far-fetched and kind of ridiculous.

Let me tell you a story of a young boy who loved taking apart cars and putting them back together just for the sake of it. Soaked in sweat, grease, and aching with hard labor, one day, he realized that he wants to spend his life surrounded by machines. That kick-started his love for gadgets, and he found himself mesmerized by the power and intricacy of computers. But who was he?

Steve Jobs.
The man who found Apple.
The man who made a career out of his passion and changed the world with just one idea.
The man who revolutionized the world of technology.

Not only Steve Jobs, but all those renowned figures like Walt Disney, Stephen King, and Benjamin Franklin. They started like you: mind brimming with ideas, yet the prospect of failing scared and kept them awake at night. However, they all had one thing in common. They embarked on a journey of self-discovery. There is a secret blessing in this unearthing of one's self. Life tests you in this way; it prepares you for the upcoming challenges and ensures whether you deserve the victory in that 'battle' or are you meant to be a warrior of another one. The Universe, the Eternal Being, every star in the sky and every grain of sand is with you—and within you. Help is provided to those who want to explore themselves with full heart, mind, and most importantly, soul because that is where your authentic self exists. The heart might shatter after a few setbacks. The brain might lose interest or whisper about the impossibility of the task on dead, dark nights, slowly weaving threads of self-doubt until that is who you are. But putting your soul in the search will never let you wander away or astray from your path. That is the power of your authentic self, which I would help you develop in this book.

This guide is designed to make you pause and think deeply about the answers. We do not often give ourselves the luxury of time and solitude to figure things out. But when we do, we have the power to transform our lives.

Let's break down simply what this book will cover and how it will stimulate your development.

This book is not just a self-help book. It is a manual about the journey of the heart in and out of the ocean of this life. It is a book about how to keep your heart from sinking to the dark and dreary depths of the ocean, and what to do when it does. And what to do if you have been trapped in a rusty, corroding mind for decades.

Maybe you're an ambitious high school or college graduate with big dreams and ideas but can't get your mind to focus on deciding on your one *true* passion. Maybe you're being held back by your fears, dreading big changes, and clinging to the financial security and comfort provided by your job even though it seems to drain the life out of you. Maybe you know exactly what to do but never really acting on these urges just because your parents, teachers, and peers seem to disapprove of your idea or simply because you have no idea how to plan and execute these goals. It doesn't matter if you're just starting out in your professional life or at the height of your career, either too distracted by the glint and glitter of social media to focus on changing your profession or scared of embarking in an unexplored direction, bogged down by obligations, and traditions. It doesn't matter who you are, what you're doing, or where you currently stand in your life—this book is for everyone. From those who have no idea to those who know exactly what they want but just want a nudge in the right direction—everyone can benefit from the strategies, tips, methods, and plans discussed in this book.

Don't read this book with your mind only. Try to recognize any feelings that emerge within you as you read every single line. I can't let you in on any deep philosophies or wisdom; all of these are already buried deep inside your heart. All I can do is to remind you of what you have ignored—your true potential. Living knowledge, ancient and ever new, is then activated and released from every cell in your body. It was written based on the accumulated experiences and exhaustive research to help us discover our true selves. You will see things you have already seen, yet you have never truly seen. You will realize that something profoundly significant has happened to you. There is then a feeling of euphoria and heightened aliveness, as something within you says: "Yes, this is my one true passion!"

Over the years, as a business and personal coach consultant, I have helped hundreds of individuals and entrepreneurs achieve personal happiness and business success. Helping people to be happier, seeing a smile on their faces, and bridging the gap between them and success—*this* is my passion. Not finding their passion or their destined greatness has been a common issue that I have been trying to help people with over the years. I have researched, tested multiple strategies, and applied unique methodologies before writing this book so it can be effective for everyone and anyone around the globe. I want to spread the words and show people that it is not hard to find their passion, which can be developed into a lifelong career or business.

In this book, you will find out how to leverage the power of the questions to the one thing that you are meant to be focusing on. You will learn how to tranf0rk your life now so that you can more easily create the future—your future—your way—your reality—your universe and your life. Once you get on the right track, dealing with things like being addicted to entertainment or a life of mediocrity will be a thing of the past. You will get up every day with a bounce in your step and an eagerness for life that you never had before…

Are you ready to destroy all of those limiting blocks you have right now and dive right in?

Great! Let's go. And do yourself a favor by really putting in the time it's going to take in order to become more clear and to follow your true passion in life. Once you figure it out, then all you have to do is to FOCUS on it, and you will create it.

So, whether your dream is to become a rock star, a doctor, a lawyer, the next Elon Musk, or the next Nikola Tesla, determine RIGHT HERE AND RIGHT NOW that you're going to figure out first what you want to be written on your tombstone. And determine RIGHT HERE AND RIGHT NOW that you're going to give it your absolute best shot effort—that you're going to do all you can to create yourself to be the person who you truly want to be.

It is just a few steps away. This is my passion, and I'm here to help you find yours.

Chapter 1

Where Are You Now? Find Yourself Through Self-Diagnostic Tools!

Picture this: you've come home after a long day at work, ready to kick back and unwind but find yourself in a miserable mood, annoyed at everything, simply unable to relax. You brush it off because you think this is normal; in your mind, *everyone* feels like this at the end of a tiring workday. What you refuse to acknowledge is that your exhaustion doesn't stem solely from working hard all day long—maybe it's more than feeling tired, maybe it's a combination of fatigue and *frustration*.

Figuring out that this exhaustion is caused by discontentment and unhappiness isn't enough. To change the course of action, you need to figure out *why* you feel unfulfilled at the end of the day. Most people refuse to address this feeling simply because they cannot be honest with themselves; you might be holding yourself back because you're afraid that confronting this dissatisfaction would mean opening yourself up to change, disapproval, financial crises, and unwavering commitment. The only way to walk through the maze in your mind is to reflect and ask yourself one fundamental question.

Why Am I Unhappy Right Now?

Let's see what the answers are.

- The way we are brought up to think about professional happiness is wrong

One reason why we fail to reach our full potential is the environment in which we're brought up; happiness in today's world is defined in monetary terms—we are raised to believe that achieving financial security will solve all our problems and will bring us unlimited joy and satisfaction. This false belief not only dilutes the idea of passion but also makes us think that professional happiness is directly linked to wealth. As a result, you put a lot of effort and energy into making yourself feel happy at a job that does not hone your skill-set or challenge you, simply because it pays well. Think of a hamster spinning on a wheel in a cage, exerting itself but not achieving anything in return. However, unlike our hypothetical hamster, you have the capacity to *think* and make a different decision that will benefit you immensely. Unless you understand that wealth and satisfaction are not intertwined with each other and that you need to unlearn these ideas that you grew up with, you will remain trapped in this never-ending, exhausting cycle.

- Undue pressure from parents

Part of this narrative is propagated by people within your immediate environment, most notably, your parents and teachers who made it seem like work and fun are on two opposite ends of the spectrum. Children learn from observation and imitation; if their parents are trapped in the jobs they don't love because it's nowhere close to their passion, they will undoubtedly sense that their parents are exhausted at the end of the day and deduce that work is supposed to be tedious, boring, and tiresome. Consequently, they enter adulthood, believing that their professional life cannot bring them any kind of pleasure, which gives birth to a thought pattern that is extremely damaging—*you cannot make a profit doing what you love.*

Parents, though well-intentioned, pressurize you to find a passion that fits within their definition of appropriate because they think they know what kind of jobs can make you a good living, and your passion may not fall into those categories. This leads to most individuals either shying away from pursuing their goals or molding their ambitions to the standards set by society. If you allow your choices to be dictated by your surroundings, you will end up deceiving yourself into jobs, dreams, and goals that aren't in line with what you truly *want*, deep down.

- School desensitizes us to passions

Let's talk about the education system and its undue emphasis on uniformity; instead of teaching students to embrace their individuality, most of the schools try to have the students work on the same tasks and goals, which leads to them becoming indistinguishable from one another in the way they are thinking. This attempt to fit everyone within the same box and to admonish those who try to explore new avenues is especially harmful as it actively discourages individuals from pursuing their goals. The truth is that little training or knowledge, which can help them get in touch with their passion, is provided to students prior to their admission to college. Consequently, this lack of awareness results in one of two possibilities: either they choose their major based on their parents' advice or pick subjects which they consider to be lucrative in the future.

Unfortunately, this plan rarely yields viable results because you end up choosing a major that doesn't align with your dreams and ambitions, even if it is highly profitable.

If students were encouraged to acknowledge, celebrate, and utilize their unique traits, skills, and personalities to find their passion, more people would feel comfortable in thinking about what they truly want out of their professional life.

Schools also end up desensitizing students to passion by shifting their focus from personal and professional development to grades and scores from a very young age. This highly structured routine leaves them with little time to experiment and think about their passion. Even the fixed curriculum is designed to prepare students for a specific set of jobs, which means that those who wish to follow unconventional careers are placed at an automatic disadvantage. Everything is a competition, and those who cannot keep up are offered little support or encouragement.

If you felt like you could relate to any of the above reasons, it's highly likely that you've found an explanation for your feelings. However, your self-reflection does not stop at just figuring out *why* you're dissatisfied with your circumstances. Think of this chapter as an extensive questionnaire that will reveal important details about your current emotional health, personality, and fears. It will serve as the foundation of your blueprint to passion; the key to the map which you will construct by clearing the first, probably the hardest stage of all—self-reflection and assessment.

Why Is It Important To Get In Touch With Yourself?

You might be wondering *why* it's so important to just sit back and think about who you are and what you want. After all, you've probably already spent countless hours thinking on the subject and did not find any answers. The problem is that unstructured thinking, obstructed by fears, anxieties, and unrealistic expectations rarely yield any results since you indulge in the exercise either out of self-pity or fear. The objective of this chapter is to help you get into a headspace that is devoid of these imaginary shackles so that you can find concrete answers. Remember, this will be a fruitful endeavor if you decide to be honest with yourself, regardless of its temporary emotional toll. It is essential that you find time to get in touch with your authentic self—the part of your personality that is focused on *your* needs, wants, and goals, free from the pressures exerted by family, friends, peers, and society—because it will be the sole decider of what your passion actually is.

Here are three reasons why it's essential to reach out to your authentic self:

- Self-awareness is key to mental health

One reason why this task is absolutely necessary for both personal and professional growth as it generates self-awareness, which plays a significant part in finding your passion. Without this comprehension of the self, you will find yourself succumbing to the expectations of others around you and saying yes to every opportunity that comes your way because you do not have a solid understanding of who you are when all external descriptors are removed.

Individuals who depend on other people, events, and objects to define their personality are vulnerable to self-deprecation, anxiety, and unhappiness as they fail to ground themselves in reality. As a result, these individuals are easily demotivated, define themselves in terms of their relationships with others, have a difficult time dealing with their emotions, and are quick to assume that they are bound to fail every time just because it happened once.

- It is not a selfish endeavor

Make no mistake, focusing on your personal growth and health is the opposite of selfish; only if you begin to understand yourself will you become a productive, happy individual that can contribute the best of yourself to society. Those who fail to put their emotional health above everything else often find themselves lashing at the people around them because they do not have the tools or coping mechanisms to deal with their feelings.

One way you can accomplish this is by sitting down at the end of every day and talking aloud to yourself like you would do with a friend. Ask yourself this: *how am I feeling right now?* Once you've identified each separate feeling, proceed to figure out which event in your day might have caused these emotions. In this way, you're able to process your negative emotions in a healthy manner; those who do not hold regular conversations with themselves are prone to frequent outbursts, which are a direct result of repression and accumulation of negative thoughts.

- Mental health affects physical health

Due to a lack of awareness surrounding mental well-being makes us believe that bad mental health only manifests itself in the form of self-defeating thought patterns. This couldn't be farther from the truth. Regularly dismissing negative emotions can lead to a deterioration of physical health as the two are closely intertwined. In fact, one of the first symptoms of declining emotional health is somatic rather than psychological. This means that people who are unaware of the stress, pressure, anxiety, and sadness they live under are more likely to experience headaches, chronic pain in different areas of the body, and other physiological problems. Since such people are unaware of their emotional state and usually repress any negative feeling, their mind tries to warn them through a different route by provoking the body to exhibit an abnormal, biological response. If you constantly feel tired, suffer from aches in the head, stomach, joints, and back, you might want to consider using the aforementioned techniques to sort out your emotions.

Self-diagnostics Through Checklists

The prospect of change can be daunting for anyone. The first mistake that you can make is to push yourself to take on big projects and tasks, without any prior research about who you are as a person. In this section, we'll take a look at four checklists which will help you identify your priorities, values, habits, and various different traits. Your task is to be completely truthful while filling out each checklist so that you can better understand yourself!

- Worksheet 1—What Have You Stopped Doing That You Wish You Were

This checklist was developed by Dr. Chris Williams, Emeritus Professor of Psychosocial Psychiatry at the University of Glasgow, for Living Life to the Full—a website designed to help people in attaining their goals and living their best life. Dr. Williams is a licensed CBT practitioner who specializes in education. Your task is to think about all the activities that you used to enjoy but haven't been doing lately and create an ideal, balanced daily and weekly routine for yourself by answering the questions given below.

Fun/pleasure

- ❏ Enjoying sport (watching or taking part)
- ❏ Enjoying music/attending shows and concerts
- ❏ Watching a film/going to the cinema
- ❏ Doing a hobby
- ❏ Watching TV
- ❏ Going out in nature for a walk
- ❏ Doing exercise/swimming/running/gym
- ❏ Reading a good book, magazine or podcast
- ❏ Practicing relaxation techniques/yoga/pilates

Getting things done/achievement:

- ❏ Learning something new/class
- ❏ Learning to play a new musical instrument

- ❏ Planning and cooking regular meals
- ❏ Making your house look good (ironing, cleaning, tidying)

Spending time with people you like/Closeness:

- ❏ Seeing your friends, relatives or people you like
- ❏ Phoning or texting friends/keeping in touch with others
- ❏ Going to church, mosque, temple or synagogue if that's important to you
- ❏ Going to a club or supporting your team with others

Routine:

- ❏ Spending time with your pets (e.g. walking the dog)
- ❏ Keeping to regular mealtimes
- ❏ Keeping up with the garden/looking after house plants that give color to your life

To get closer to your authentic self, you will need to figure out why you're no longer doing the activities that you used to enjoy immensely. Once you begin thinking about the reasons for your detachment, you'll understand the importance of creating a routine that includes all the things that you find joy in. Integrating these activities into your schedule can help you relax, unwind, and find happiness; all of these emotions will help you find your true self!

- Worksheet 2—Clarifying Values and Making Life Changes

The following checklists have been taken from the first chapter of Russ Harris' book, *The Confidence Gap*. Read through all the questions and carefully think about each one before you begin to write any answers down. It is highly likely that you will see many common themes in all your answers, this points towards the fundamental values that you hold close to your heart and highlight areas where you need to improve your confidence.

In a universe where you suddenly immeasurable confidence:

- What would change about your behavior?
- What would change about the way you work and play?
- What would change about the way you treat your friends, relatives, partner, parents, children, and work colleagues?
- What would change about the way you talk to yourself? Would you treat your mind and body differently?
- What would change about your character?
- What kind of activities would you begin doing?
- What activities would you stop taking part in?
- How would your goals change, and what approach will you take to accomplish them?
- What contrasts would you observe in your relationships?
- How would your unlimited confidence help you change the world?

As I gain actual confidence

- These are some ways in which I will behave differently:
- These are the ways in which I will act towards others differently:
- These are some ways in which I will behave towards myself:
- Here are some traits and strengths I will gain:
- These are the ways in which I will act differently in my relationships with friends and family:
- These are the ways in which I will act differently in my relationships that revolve around my career, education, and leisure
- These are some important values I will live by:
- These are the activities I will start to do:
- These are my goals:

- These are some immediate actions I will take to enhance my routine:

The main purpose here is to help you clarify your values. These two sets of questions define the kind of persona you hope to be like. The first checklist gives you an idea of the goals, values, and traits that you wish to adopt in the future, while the second set of questions enables you to define the activities, actions, and behaviors that you can integrate in your daily routine as you build up your confidence.

- Worksheet 3—Rate Your Values

The following checklist was also created by Russ Harris (2011) and can be found at www.thehappinesstrap.com. It will help you understand how you want to think and behave throughout your lifetime. Everyone has different values; it's somewhat like your taste in food and differs widely across people, cultures, and environments.

Your job is to rate each of the 58 listed values as V = very important, Q = quite important, and N = not so important. Ensure that at least ten of the enlisted values are marked as V = very important. Once you've gone through the entire checklist, write down the ten values that you marked as *very important*, separately. Select six of these that you feel strongly about and write them down on a sheet of paper. This will help you remember what's important to you and the code with which you want to live your life. If you feel that there are significant values missing, you can insert them in the space yourself.

1. Acceptance: to be open-minded and to accept life, people, and myself
2. Adventure: to seek and create new and interesting experiences
3. Assertiveness: to respectfully create boundaries in personal and professional life by standing up for what I want and deserve
4. Authenticity: to be true to my authentic self

5. Beauty: to cherish, seek, care for or create beauty in my own self, other people, and nature, etc
6. Caring: to nurture myself, other people, the environment, etc
7. Challenge: to develop, improve, and learn by challenging myself
8. Compassion: to be kind to everyone, especially those who are suffering
9. Connection: to immerse myself fully in any activity I'm doing, and be mindful and grounded in the present with others
10. Contribution: to help others and myself in making a positive change in the world
11. Conformity: to respect and obey the law and its rules
12. Cooperation: to amiably collaborate with other people
13. Courage: to be valiant and brave; to be resilient during moments of fear and adversity
14. Creativity: to be innovative and think out of the box
15. Curiosity: to be curious about the world and those that live in it
16. Encouragement: to appreciate values that I respect in myself or other individuals
17. Equality: to treat people fairly, without any discrimination or bias
18. Excitement: to seek, create and participate in activities that I find thrilling
19. Fairness: to be just in my dealings with others and myself
20. Fitness: to enhance my physical and mental health; to improve my fitness
21. Flexibility: to acclimate and adapt quickly to change
22. Freedom: to exist freely; to have the autonomy to make my own decisions
23. Friendliness: to be amiable and nice towards other people
24. Forgiveness: to be forbearing to others and myself
25. Fun: to create and spread fun and cheer and take part in activities that amuse me
26. Generosity: to share and give to others without feeling any negative emotion
27. Gratitude: to be thankful to myself, my life, and other people

28. Honesty: to be truthful and honest with other people and myself.
29. Humour: to seek and value the funny moments in life
30. Humility: to be humble and not let my boasting overshadow my actions
31. Industry: to dedicate myself to working hard
32. Independence: to be autonomous, and live without dependence on anyone else
33. Intimacy: to open up emotionally or physically and share myself in my relationships
34. Justice: to stand by what is right and fair
35. Kindness: to be compassionate and kind towards other people and myself
36. Love: to be affectionate with other people and myself
37. Mindfulness: to be grounded in the present reality, at all times
38. Order: to be organized and maintain a healthy order in life
39. Open-mindedness: to engage in a healthy discussion with people who have a different world view, and allow my perception to be changed based on the fairly weighted evidence.
40. Patience: to wait without creating a fuss for the things that I want in life
41. Persistence: to soldier on and remain resolute in the face of adversity
42. Pleasure: to seek pleasure and give it to other people and myself
43. Power: to take charge and lead if necessary
44. Reciprocity: to create strong, healthy relationships in which there is a balance of giving and taking
45. Respect: to be considerate of other people and my own feelings and behaviors; be polite and respectful to others
46. Responsibility: to be reliable and fulfill all duties to the best of my ability
47. Romance: to show and express affection and love
48. Safety: to ensure the safety of myself and those around me

49. Self-awareness: to acknowledge and be aware of my thoughts, emotions, and actions
50. Self-care: to nourish myself and care for my wellbeing
51. Self-development: to keep learning and improving skills, knowledge and specialties.
52. Self-control: to uphold my ideals and values
53. Sensuality: to seek and gain pleasure from experiences that engage all five senses
54. Sexuality: to think about and express my sexuality
55. Spirituality: to bind myself to causes and entities that are larger than myself
56. Skillfulness: to develop and practice my skills and seek experiences to enhance them
57. Supportiveness: to be helpful and supportive; to encourage and help others in living their best life
58. Trust: to be loyal, sincere, and trustworthy in all my dealings
59. Insert your own values that not listed here:

This checklist helps you rate your values and prioritize them. You can easily pick out the features and aspects that you value the most.

Once you've finished going through all the checklists, print out the answers to each and pin them up so that you can regularly read and review what you want to do and the kind of person you wish to become. These core values serve as reminders, reinforcing your goals and helping you create a plan to achieve them; once you begin to visualize this as your reality, you will find it easy to keep track of all your goals.

Self-diagnostic Through Journaling

Journaling is another great approach towards figuring out your priorities, values, passions, and goals. Research studies have demonstrated the usefulness of journaling; it enables people to develop a healthy coping mechanism to deal with stress, anxiety, depression and even enhances the body's immune response. Neurologist Judy Willis, MD, claims that "The practice of writing can enhance the brain's intake, processing, retaining, and retrieving of information… it promotes the brain's attentive focus … boosts long-term memory, illuminates patterns, gives the brain time for reflection, and when well-guided, is a source of conceptual development and stimulus of the brain's highest cognition" (Willis, 2011).

In case you're overwhelmed and don't know where to start, I have included four highly effective journal prompts that can get you back on track. During this stage, you might feel swamped by the thoughts buzzing around in your head, pulling you in different directions. The best way to cross this bridge is to take a pen and paper, sit down in a quiet room, and sort this mess by writing your heart out.

- Mission Statement

Remember how you picked your top six values in Worksheet 3? Well, it's time to put those results to use. A mission statement is basically a paragraph that details an organization's goals, purpose, core value, target audience, and the services provided by it. Your task is to write a similar statement that outlines your current goal, your expertise, value, and why you want to pursue a particular passion. Make full use of the insights that you've gained so far in this chapter to fill these four headings. This motto will remind you of your direction in life, even on bleak, purposeless days.

For example, this is Oprah Winfrey's personal mission statement:

"To be a teacher. And to be known for inspiring my students to be more than they thought they could be."

Oprah Winfrey's mission statement encompasses all four elements that are essential to a mission statement: her goal (to be known as an inspiration), purpose (to teach), target audience (students), and value (to inspire and help others).

Another short example is the mission statement of author, activist, and poet, Maya Angelou:

"To serve as a leader, live a balanced life, and apply ethical principles to make a significant difference."

You can use these as a starting point to create a phrase that summarizes the meaning and purpose of your life.

- Circle of Loves

Get ready for a little drawing exercise!

Draw a huge circle in the middle of a blank page. All you need to do is fill this circle in with all the things that you love, cherish, and desire. They don't have to be big goals or aspirations; you can start with the simplest of pleasures like coffee, pizza, cycling, beach, your dream coffee shop, etc. Build your way up to more complex things and experiences. Keep going until the circle is completely filled, and you can't come up with more things to put in. This is supposed to be a visual representation of what you want in life; make sure that you circle the ones that appeal the most to your heart and mind! When you direct your focus to the essential, you manage to get rid of what's unimportant. If you made a circle of loves, what would you put down in it? Here is an example of it.

- Are/Should Be/Would Rather Exercise

Draw three columns and label them 'Are', 'Should Be', and 'Would Rather'. This task is pretty self-explanatory; all you have to do is assess your current lifestyle to see whether you're on the right track by writing about things that you're currently doing, activities that you should be doing, and things that you would rather spend time doing. The 'are' should comprise of things that you're occupied with; the 'should be' should be a list of activities that you *think* you should be doing, while the 'would be' column should contain all the things that bring you happiness. The table looks like the following one.

Are	Should Be	Would Rather
• Using social media all day long • Playing video games and watch Netflix • Work on my current tedious job	• Prepare for my law school entrance exams • Get my homework finished • Looking for other jobs that seem more interested to me	• Start a sustainable, environment-friendly fashion brand • Learn a new musical instrument such as piano • Start my own business such as a restaurant, a bar or an IT company

- Top 25 Wants Exercise

Now they have answered three checklists and got a journal to write. You might be tired and tempted to stop here. The following exercise may take you some willpower to do, but it is worth the effort. Would you rather spend your entire life going through the pain of a purposeless existence, watching people around you achieve their wildest dreams while you're still stuck, struggling to figure things out? You want to change, right?

Shake things up with another journal prompt and push yourself through to the finish line.

Write down twenty-five things that you would love to have in your life. Think as creatively as you can! A perfect partner in life? Do you want to live in a beach house or house on the top of a mountain? Do you want to be debt-free and wealthy? Do you want a happy family with a couple of lovely kids? Do you want to be respected and known for the things you are doing? Where do you want to travel? Do you want an adorable dog, cat, or other pets? Do you want a career that you can devote your whole life to, just like Kobe Bryant and Michael Jordan? Keep going until you have around 25 things on your list. Once this is done, start slashing until you're left with five things that you simply can't imagine your life without. Through this exercise, you will learn to redirect your concentration to your priorities, instead of letting your mind wander around, thinking of all possibilities. Remember, the objective is to achieve clarity, and nothing is quite as effective as weeding out the non-essential desires that have been clouding your better judgment.

Self-diagnostic Through Projects: Creating A Dream Board To Visualize Your Wildest Ambitions

The next step is to create a dream board. Once you have done all your exercises above, you should be able to pick up your top 5 desires, no matter they are about wealth, health, or relationship. Now, you can create this dream board to visualize what you want in life. It will be more powerful if you can use pictures on your vision board instead of pure words. One celebrity who attests to the power of a dream board is comedian, Ellen DeGeneres, who often talks about how she made a dream board to achieve one of her life goals; to appear on the cover of O Magazine, founded by Oprah Winfrey. Other famous personalities include John Assaraf, Sonja Fisher, Lilly Singh, Steve Harvey, Shay Mitchell, and Patrick Starr. By looking at the board every day and remind yourself of the things you really want will help you get there much faster than without having it.

Self-diagnostic Through Personality Tests

Let's take a look at another technique through which you can explore your true self: personality tests. A lot of personality tests are available on the internet, but I would personally recommend the Myers-Briggs Personality Test as it is perfect for those who want a detailed analysis of their personality type, approach to relationships, recommended career options and preferences. It provides you with a holistic and atomistic evaluation rather than just giving you a label. Inspired by the theories of the prominent psychoanalyst, Carl Jung and developed by Katharine Cook Briggs and Isabel Briggs Myers; the test consists of an extensive questionnaire that expands your awareness of who you are and how you should approach life. The test can be accessed through the internet; simply go to your search browser and type in the name of the test to get started right now!

Going through all the questionnaires, exercises, and tasks is not easy. You've taken the first steps in the right direction! In this chapter, we analyzed the three reasons why you do not feel fulfilled right now and explored various self-diagnostic tools to get in touch with what we really desire. The first checklist in the "Self-diagnostics through checklists", enabled us to realize the importance of maintaining a healthy and happy life routine. Going through worksheets 2 and 3, we clarified and rated our values. We also covered techniques such as journaling and creating a dream board to help you stick to your goals. Don't let this momentum go to waste and read on to discover how you can begin your journey towards a fulfilling, passionate life by saying the word 'no'.

Chapter 2

What You Don't Want: Setting Boundaries In Your Professional Life

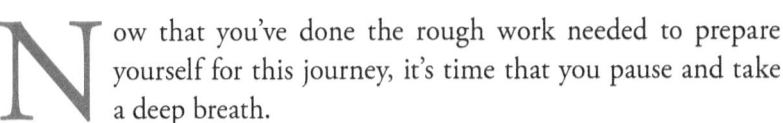

Now that you've done the rough work needed to prepare yourself for this journey, it's time that you pause and take a deep breath.

It's highly probable that you've discovered some truly shocking things about yourself by this point; more often than not, the element of surprise stems from your inability to *know* yourself because you realize that the things being revealed have been in front of you the entire time. However, treat this self-awareness like a double-edged sword; the personal discoveries you've made from the tests given in the previous chapter might end up adding several different passions to your list. In order to bridge the gap between clarity and action, I will show you various ways in which you can create a comprehensive list of things you do *not* want to end up doing and different methods by which you can avoid such situations. All you need is a quiet place where you can get into a headspace that allows you to honestly analyze each option; remember, the ultimate trick to getting in touch with the candid, authentic part of yourself is to ask structured, open-ended questions! Once you achieve the ability to generate these questions without any help, you will find yourself one step closer to the finish line.

Most people think they want money and don't realize that money does not have any inherent value or meaning. Most of the things people enjoy doing don't necessarily bring them wealth, but why they like doing it. Consequently, they end up chasing the wrong things in life, simply because they are unclear about what they *don't* want. You want to get into a headspace that allows you to be honest with yourself. The aim of this chapter is to help you get to that point!

Examine Your Whys To Figure Out Which Wants Aren't Really Wants At All

One way in which you can save yourself from this disappointment is to have a conversation with yourself based on the 5 Whys rule.

Review your answers to the journaling and checklist exercises in the previous chapter to visualize all the things that you truly want in life. Your task is to find a reason for each desire. You might feel as if you know the answer, but when you begin to pen down each cause, you will find yourself unraveling a deeper mystery. Take ten minutes to find out one reason why you might want to change your circumstances; maybe you want to travel more or do something financially rewarding, or maybe you feel as if you're stuck in an endless loop that is emotionally and mentally draining. Once you have pinpointed the exact reason, ask yourself—*why is that?* Why do you want to travel more? Why do you want to earn more? Why do you feel emotionally exhausted every day? Keep at this exercise of analyzing each cause in turn until you've repeated the same question five times. The conclusion will be sure to surprise you.

Maybe you thought you desired a higher income because you really wanted to travel and expand your horizons, but in the process of asking yourself *why*, you realized something deeper. You discovered that you're unhappy at your current job not because it prevents you from traveling but because you feel that the emotional payback isn't enough. This is the kind of breakthrough which helps you be honest with the biggest stakeholder in this situation—*you!*

The idea behind the prompt is simple; it is designed to help you confront your desires and to look for the reasons that drive you towards achieving a specific goal. The target is to uncover the uncomfortable truth and find the *real* solution for your problem, not the one that you *think* will work; in the scenario presented above, it was discovered that the solution wasn't to travel frequently but to change professional routes to find something that is both challenging and fulfilling. This exercise will not only help you challenge your beliefs but will also help you distinguish between real and artificial wants. After all, the idea is to question yourself instead of settling for familiar, comforting conclusions. Your belief-system might just crash, but take heart, the rubble will help you build a steadier foundation on which you can base your passion.

Get Rid Of The Shoulds That Don't Add Up With Your Wants

Let's circle back to why a lot of people fail to make a real change in their professional lives even when they realize that their current circumstances are nothing but a dead-end.

One fear that's most common among all these people is that they're bogged down by *shoulds*.

You might be unwilling to change paths because you think you *should* do something that's profitable. You *should* choose a career that is acceptable to your parents. A job that *should* be able to support your needs. I believe that this logic-based approach is flawed for several reasons. Firstly, it blinds you to reality and makes it very hard to prioritize desire and want. As we discussed in the previous chapter, a lot of this conflict stems from the idea that work and fun are polar opposites. Once you stop valuing rationalization so much, you realize that finding your passion is not supposed to be based on facts and figures but on what works for you as an individual. The idea is to free yourself from expectations, the ones that others impose on you, and the ones that you have of yourself. After all, these *shoulds* are nothing more than a blindfold, meant to trap you within an unfulfilling career, deceiving your mind into thinking that you're doing the right thing. Beware, doing the right thing is not the same as doing the thing you *want*. To find your passion, you need to get rid of the shoulds that do not fit into the whys you discovered in the last section and gain some perspective on what you've been held back by all your life.

A lot of people ask the same question—why are these *shoulds* so terrible? Isn't it better to make decisions that are driven by reason and rationale?

No. At least not the way we're taught.

You see, years of indoctrination and desensitization have forced us to think that our wants should align with these *shoulds*. Over time, you find yourself so deeply immersed in these expectations that you confuse them with passion. Consequently, your desires melt into the background of your mind and stop talking to you. Most people think of their childhood as the best time of their lives, and that's because children refuse to keep their heads down, walk the line, and accommodate *shoulds* in their life. They take bold risks and do what they love until their environment begins to exert its pressure and changes them into a watered-down version of who they really are. It becomes especially harmful when these *shoulds* sever the connection you had with your authentic self, essentially reducing you to an intelligent machine that behaves in expected, safe and predictable ways. The problem is that these expectations and pressures force you to fit within a small box, with no regard for your shape or size, chipping away at your edges, dimming your passion until you barely recognize yourself. You feel miserable, sick, and sad, but you can't find your way back to your true identity because it has been smothered by these *shoulds*.

I know this because I felt the same way once and decided that I couldn't go on putting up a facade to please these *shoulds*.

Sit down and think about why you're pursuing a particular job. Is it because you *want* to or because you *should*? Remember that these *shoulds* often disguise themselves to trick you; you might feel as if you *need* to do something or that you simply *have* to pursue a particular career. You also might have difficulty envisioning yourself without these trappings because change can be daunting, but it's important that you silence these doubts and think about how your goals align with these external expectations. Once you manage to sift through the remnants of these chains, you'll realize that you've been misled in your quest for passion. You'll discover that you've been trying to fit the pieces of a puzzle the wrong way; even though your mind will try to resist and tell you to stick to familiar paths, the only way you can overcome this dissatisfaction is if you venture outside the box that you've been caged in. Get rid of all the *shoulds* which are not in line with your ambitions, and you'll discover the sheer number of expectations that do not add up to your passion. Your life is not supposed to be an endless parade of shoulds, don't let yourself be duped into this classic trap!

Exercises To Find Out What Wastes Your Time

There are several ways that you can identify the distractors which prevent you from making a commitment to your ambitions. One effective technique to keep track of all these thought patterns is to turn to journaling so that you have a written record that helps you identify all areas that distract you and waste your time. You might say that it's enough to just *think* about what you want, but it's nearly impossible to reach any solid conclusions until and unless you look at what you've written. It grounds you in reality and activates your memory to pay attention to similar signs in everyday life. Use the following questions to begin this simple journaling exercise.

- What stresses you out?

Do you like watching Netflix and play video games? Do you think doing things like that all day long makes you relaxed or eventually stresses you out? Do you feel fulfilled after playing video games all day long or a bit anxious since you wasted so much time on it? Write down a list about things that seem to entertain you but actually stresses you.

Regarding your career, what part of your job makes you anxious and prevents you from reaching your full potential? Is it your career choice itself, your current job, or some aspect related to it? Make a list of the different stressors and try to write down why each one bothers you. Are you stressed out by tight deadlines, long working hours, being micromanaged, or low chances of being promoted to a leading position?

This task allows you to take some action and progress from the passive, emotional to an active, solution-oriented stage.

- Who annoys you?

Is it your boss and colleagues, or does the issue run deeper than just minor disagreements that are bound to occur in an office setting? Chances are, you'll find yourself annoyed with *what* you're doing rather than those you're doing it with if you're pursuing the wrong career path. Is it your friends or family who demand constant attention and emotional energy, asking you to devote all of your time to being with them? Vocalizing these grievances and writing them down will help you figure out where the problem stems from. You cannot treat a disease unless you eliminate all possible causes—similarly, in order to find your passion, you need to weed out all things that are making you unhappy, tired, and unfulfilled. Try to think of this journaling exercise as a meditation rather than viewing your complaints as ungrateful. What you're trying to achieve here is simple; you want to do something with your life that not only makes you *want* to leap out of bed every morning but also helps you self-actualize. None of it will be possible unless you learn to control and process your emotions.

- What do you pretend to like?

The next step in this exercise is to think about all the features of your current routine that you only *pretend* to like. Maybe your friends want you to watch a movie with them, but you would rather stay at home and get some work done? Remember when we talked about the infamous *shoulds*? Refer to your knowledge of this cunning inner voice and try to find out what you've only been pretending to enjoy just because someone expects you to. This will give you further clarity in knowing what to absolutely avoid in your next career decision, helping you choose your one, true calling from a hundred good ideas. Without putting down your mask, giving up this act, and looking deep into yourself, you will not be able to get away from the voice of the *shoulds*.

- What is it about your past or current job that you would never want to do again?

The last question in this exercise will give you a complete report on how you feel about your career. When you begin to pen this down, make sure that you leave notes on why you would never wish to go through it again. Was it tedious, unchallenging, difficult, dishonest, or did it make you feel as if you're a failure? In this way, you will be able to ground each point into a tangible feeling, event, and thought, which will be immensely beneficial once you begin thinking about the various careers that you could choose. It will also help you steer clear of all jobs that sound similar to the ones you hated so that you can never fall back into the same trap ever again.

Dedicate a considerable amount of time to finishing this task so that you have a list of requirements and desires before you can move onto a job hunt as this portion will be fundamental to the blueprint needed for finding your life's passion.

How To Say No

The previous exercise should have enabled you to find out what you don't want in your life. Now, it's time that you put your feelings into words by saying no to these things!

Let's start with small actions that you can take; the easiest way to say no is to use certain linguistic strategies that make it easier for you to navigate tricky situations.

- Avoid apologies but give thank yous

Instead of apologizing for turning down a project at work or saying no to a plan with your friends, say thank you. This simple trick manages to make you sound empathetic as you draw boundaries.

For example: *'Thank you for offering me the opportunity to lead this project, but I'm swamped with other tasks and will not be able to manage the workload.'*

Similarly, in case you're cornered into a situation which doesn't quite feel right, use the 'it's not you, it's me' phrase to express yourself. For instance, if someone wants to collaborate with you on a project, but you don't feel as if it is for you, just tell them that while it might not work for you, it'd be perfect for someone else.

- Use alternatives to 'no' that means 'no'

If you don't want to say the word 'no' but want to get the point across, there are several alternate phrases you can use.

One way to avoid saying the word no is to replace it with a phrase like "let me think about it". For example, if someone wants you to help them through something, but you have prior commitments or are tied up at work, you can say something like: *'I understand. Let me think about it'*. If you don't give further responses, people will know that this means "no".

You can also indirectly compliment the other person to say no in a professional setting. For example: *'I think you are more qualified to handle this project than me!'*

- Use body language to get your point across

Body language can also be used to communicate the same point without even having to use words. Shake your head, smile ruefully, and gesticulate with your hands to show that you're not going to say yes.

- Don't offer unnecessary explanations

Now that we've taken a glance at the different ways in which you can twist your words to say no in delicate situations. Don't jump to offer explanations unless it is absolutely necessary. Frequently, we think that the only way we can get off the hook is by giving long-winded explanations and reasons. However, this can make your words sound insincere and prompt the other person to offer solutions to whatever reason you come up, which puts you in a very awkward position.

For example, your friends are planning to have dinner at the weekend, but you want to stay at home and enjoy your day off work. You say no to the plans and back up your words with multiple reasons for why you can't come along. Maybe you tell them that you have a lot of work to catch up on or that you don't feel well enough for a night out. There's a high chance that your friends will keep pushing you to go out with them because you were not direct enough in your approach.

- What to do when you're caught off-guard?

Most of the time, you can predict these situations. After all, you saw your friends planning a night out in the group chat and knew that they were going to ask you to accompany them. You know it's coming, and you're prepared.

But what to do when you're caught completely off guard?

Use these two classic phrases and buy yourself some time to think of a suitable explanation: *'Oh I see, well I'll get back to you once I check my schedule'* or *'I'm not certain if that's entirely possible, right now—but I'll get back to you.'*

- Repetition

The only way to master this useful skill is through constant practice.

Start today. Say no to one thing that doesn't add happiness and satisfaction to your life. It doesn't have to be a big step; your task is to build up your resilience until you're not afraid of saying no to things that do not align with your core values.

The key is to practice this skill until you can easily maneuver your way out of social and professional situations that encroach on your personal time, goals, routine, and mental health.

It takes some getting used to, but unless you step out of your comfort zone, you'll never be able to break out of your bubble and confront your true passion! The aim of this chapter was to help you break free from the *shoulds* in life and confront what you don't want. Furthermore, we also learned certain techniques to say no to these things so that you can use that time and energy to work on what you love and desire. Of course, making all these changes to your lifestyle can seem daunting and uncomfortable; the next chapter will deal with the biggest hurdle in your path to passion—your fears.

Chapter 3

The Ultimate Guide To Facing Your Fears

So far, you've identified your desires, values, goals, and what you don't want in life. But have you ever wondered *why you* are not doing what you want to be doing or *why* you are still doing what you don't want to be doing? Are you being held back by your fear?

So how would you define fear?

People don't believe me when I tell them that this particular sensation is perhaps the most misunderstood one of all feelings. They think that their understanding of fear is solid and true because of all the times they've experienced it first-hand.

You know how it goes—the shaky legs, the sweaty palms, the erratic heartbeat thundering in your ears, that terrifying feeling of wanting to run but finding it hard to move your limbs and so on. Fear is universal, we have all felt it at some point in our lives at varying intensities, and so we are predisposed to think that feeling a particular emotion is the same as knowing what it is.

It's time that you sit down and re-evaluate your understanding of fear so that you can learn how to overcome the biggest hurdle in your journey to discovering your life's passion. This chapter will help you understand and identify the aspects of your current circumstances that induce fear and will equip you with the strategies needed to defeat this feeling that has stopped you from achieving your full potential.

Understanding Fear: What Is It?

So, how can we narrow down our understanding of fear and accurately define it? Let's take a look!

- Fear is neither good nor bad

Many people associate the word fear with negativity—this is the biggest misconception because fear is neither good nor bad. Feelings don't have an inherent value in themselves; they gain these labels through our interpretation of the world around us; if you can convince your mind to accept fear as an instructor rather than an enemy, you will find it much easier to deal with the emotion.

- From a scientific point of view, it exists to keep us safe

Sure, it's an extremely unpleasant emotion that sends your body in fight or flight mode, but its real purpose is to activate self-preservation and help make well-informed decisions that will keep you safe. As we all know, fear isn't restricted to a particular time, situation, object, or person; we go on about our life, carrying these fears inside us every day—fear of rejection, loneliness, failure, loss, etc. Neuroscientists assert that the human species is by far the most fearful of all existing life-forms simply because they possess the ability to think, imagine, and gain knowledge from the environment.

In short, our minds *create* fear.

It is not always triggered by external stimuli. In fact, we let ourselves fall victim to its viciousness by creating imaginary scenarios in our heads, thinking that we are somehow helping our mind preemptively deal with possible danger. So the next time you feel fearful, take a trip down memory lane and think about a time when you were extremely scared of a particular situation until you went through it, only to realize that a lot of your fear might just have been an irrational, exaggerated response, completely detached from reality.

The scientific value of fear is to keep you active; it is not meant to paralyze and freeze you till you can't function. However, that does not mean that you're supposed to jump at every opportunity and take immediate action. Once you learn to feel the emotion but not be controlled by its intensity, you will realize that it will speak to you, power your instincts and enable you to sit back, open-mindedly analyze the situation at hand and reach favorable conclusions. This ability to identify situations where it is appropriate to take immediate actions and distinguish them from instances where it's best to let your fear calm your mind is essential for anyone who wants to excel in their life.

- The FALSE Method

Let's circle back to the irrationality of fear and try to understand what we've learned so far.

One, fear is not inherently good or bad.

Two, it is an evolutionary response that is triggered by self-preservation.

The third, key component to a solid understanding of fear is acknowledging that it is irrational and exists as an illusion in our minds.

To put it simply, fear is False Evidence Appearing Real.

The FALSE Method encourages us to appreciate fear as an imaginary, non-physical entity that has no value, substance, and cannot exist outside of our minds. It is not real and has no control over you unless you choose to succumb to it. Oftentimes, we envision terrible outcomes to situations that we are scared of; however, these outcomes have no connection to reality and never materialize in real life, which means that we generate most of these in order to self-sabotage.

What Does Fear Feel Like To You?

Now that we've identified why and how fear affects us. Let's try to figure out what it may feel like for you.

All emotions are complex states of feeling, which result in certain psychological and physiological responses that are capable of affecting our behavior and cognition. The three basic features of any emotion are physiological arousal, behavior, and experience; if we ground this knowledge into what we've learned about fear, you will readily recognize that fear is a response to a certain stimulus which brings about a change in the level of hormones and neurotransmitters in the body, leading to a behavioral reaction that has the ability to change our outlook on a situation. To disentangle yourself from the damaging component of fear, it is important that you recognize the early signs. Since the cognitive component is highly subjective and is basically an aggregate of our world-views and interpretations, it cannot be objectively defined. Therefore, we turn to the physiological symptoms which are fairly universal and can be quantified, measured, and observed with ease.

Here's one easy way in which you can learn about your personalized, biological response to fear. Go through the following checklist and put a small tick next to the things that you often experience when you are afraid.

- ❏ An irregular, fast heartbeat
- ❏ An abnormal, uneven breathing pattern; your breathing is rapid, and you find yourself gasping for air
- ❏ Excessive sweating
- ❏ Sudden weakness and/or tension in muscles
- ❏ Dizziness
- ❏ Poor concentration; you cannot focus and give proper attention to your surroundings
- ❏ Pangs in the stomach
- ❏ Loss of appetite

❑ Inability to move; you find yourself frozen in terror and cannot get your limbs to function
❑ Dry mouth

This is to help you recognize your body's response so that you can process and master your fear before it takes complete control of your mind and sends you down a destructive spiral of over-thinking.

Changing Your Diet To Decrease Your Fear

- Why is diet related to anxiety/fear?

It's shocking how many people overlook the link between a good, balanced diet and decreased sensitivity to fear. Even though people seek different medical treatments and therapies to ameliorate the adverse effects of anxiety, they are unwilling to even consider changing their eating habits. This option has the power to change your life; it improves physical health, which is closely related to mental health, gives you strength, and inculcates discipline in your daily routine as you train your mind to reject instant gratification, which might harm your body in the long run. Research has linked anxiety to the levels of hormones, neurotransmitters, probiotics, and antioxidants in the body—unsurprisingly, their quantity depends on the type and amount of food items consumed on a daily basis. Therefore, it makes sense to modify your diet plan to increase the consumption of foods that alleviate any anxious feelings.

- What foods increase anxiety/fear?

Unfortunately, a lot of foods that we love eating can actually increase the intensity of our physiological response to fear. Following a balanced diet plan and drinking the required amount of water is not enough; a lot of other factors have to be taken into consideration when creating the perfect diet. Complex carbohydrates, which are found in peas, whole grains, beans, and vegetables should be included in your diet as alternatives to simple carbohydrates, found in soft drinks, candy, and various fast foods because complex carbohydrates are metabolized at a slower rate, which prevents abnormal spikes in the blood glucose levels, keeping you peaceful and tranquil. Consuming excessive amounts of simple carbohydrates in your diet causes blood glucose levels to falter, generating a response similar to the one that you experience when you're afraid. Therefore, it is important to cut down on our daily consumption of foods that contain simple carbohydrates.

The same principle applies to beverages such as coffee, as caffeine has been known to contribute to increased excitement levels as well as anxiety levels. It is important to eat unprocessed, raw foods (like carrots, celery, broccoli, etc) that do not contain sugar, caffeine, and other compounds that can induce agitation and make you anxious.

- What foods decrease anxiety?

Ninety-five percent of our body's serotonin receptors are located in the stomach lining, which further strengthens the case for the strong relationship between our diet and nervous system. The question remains—what kinds of food should be consumed to decrease the discomfort felt during fear and stress. Luckily, extensive research on mice (who are surprisingly similar to humans and share considerable physiological characteristics with them) indicated that low levels of magnesium in the body were directly related to worsening anxiety symptoms. Therefore, incorporating magnesium-rich foods such as legumes, green vegetables like spinach and chard, nuts, and whole grains within your diet can help you remain calm. Similarly, zinc reduces the intensity of anxious feelings; you can benefit from its healing powers by consuming foods like beef, egg yolk, liver, cashews, and certain seafood such as oysters. Researchers are also extremely interested in the effect of probiotics on social anxiety and recommend including foods such as pickles, kefir, and sauerkraut in your daily diet. It is also a good idea to eat foods that are rich in vitamin B, like almonds, avocados, red meat, legumes, fish, asparagus, etc, as they trigger the release of two important neurotransmitters, dopamine, and serotonin which protect you against rising anxiety levels. As mentioned above, it is also important to keep antioxidant levels in mind as they have been known to reduce anxiety and panic. Recommended food items from this category include beans (red kidney, pinto, and black), fruits (apples, cherries, plums), strawberries, blackberries, cranberries, raspberries, pecans, walnuts, broccoli, spinach, kale, turmeric, and ginger, etc.

Six Everyday Exercises To Face Fear

So far, so good.

Now that we've discussed how minor adjustments to your diet can help you overcome fear and anxiety. Let's evaluate some other techniques that will boost your resistance to fear!

Truth check: it's impossible and inadvisable to get rid of it completely. If you learn to pay attention to this feeling, it can serve as a director and guide. However, there are a few strategies you can use to prevent yourself from tumbling down the rabbit hole of fear. In this section, we will focus on six main techniques that have proven to be extremely helpful in this regard.

- Visualization exercise

Remove any distractions from your surroundings and find a serene environment in which you can practice this technique. It may take you about five minutes of guided meditation and breathing before you can set your imagination free. The idea is to fill your mind with calming, relaxing imagery that will leave no room for any negative thoughts; not only does this strategy require you to put your creative skills to use but also distracts your mind from distorting and exaggerating thought patterns that ground you in reality.

This is a famous and powerful method used to cope with panic, fear, and anxiety. It is at the base of many cognitive-behavioral therapies that aim to diminish feelings of fear by teaching individuals to broaden the creative capacity of the mind. You can visualize almost anything as long as it helps you relax; most people think about success, which enables them to formulate a mental map towards action and triumph. When you are visualizing the perfect life you desire, feel the fulfillment, happiness, peaceful it brings you as if you were living it now. Once you master this strategy, you will find yourself feeling more grounded and calm, even in the face of extreme fear.

- The 'As If' exercise

The 'As If' Method is well-known for its ability to effectively change your attitude towards fear-inducing situations. All you need to do is behave in a way that you normally would in the absence of fear; you change your facial expressions, posture, body language, and speech to reflect a calm, unafraid state of mind. Similar to visualization, this technique not only makes you *think* that you are free of fear but also encourages you to *act* that way. Assume there is a woman/man that you really want to date, but you simply can't because you're afraid of talking to them. Do it as if you are just talking to an old friend or a completely unknown person. Greet them nicely and bring up some simple topics like the weather, food, and try to strike an interesting conversation.

In this manner, you trick your mind into believing that you've gathered courage and can conquer any adversity that comes your way.

- The 'Name Your Fear' exercise

For some people, even the prospect of identifying their fear is daunting. One exercise that can benefit these types of people is known as Name Your Fears. The idea is to confront your fears by vocalizing, writing, or thinking about them. When you allow yourself to face your fears head-on, you gain strength from the mere act of being honest with yourself. If you wish to quit a job that you don't like but are held back by your fear, then write it down. This is what your list should look like:

1. No income anymore
2. No money to support the family
3. It will be difficult to pay the bills

This candid, unconventional approach is meant to reduce the negative impact of your fears by preventing repression; the more you deliberately ignore your fears and triggers, the more room they have to expand in size.

- The Emotional Freedom Technique

The ancient Chinese civilization is credited with discovering some of the most advanced medical techniques that are still in use by healthcare professionals. One such example is acupuncture, which involves pressing different spots in the body with needles so as to release trapped energy and restore the body's natural equilibrium. Emotional Freedom Tapping is a similar concept that is widely regarded as psychological acupuncture. According to its creator, Gary Craig, a lot of negative energy can accumulate at certain spots in the body leading to unequal distribution. This imbalance causes discomfort, pain, and sickness and can only be cured by using fingers to press down on *meridian points,* which basically act as centers of energy. This recalibrates the distribution of energy around the body, releasing negative and overwhelming emotions like fear. Although it is still under extensive research, experts claim that vocalization of fear combined with tapping the nine known meridian points urges neurons to fire signals at the brain, causing it to turn its attention towards stress levels. Try it now: start tapping your forehead (also known as the karate chop or small intestine meridian) while vocalizing your fear. Did you feel instantly relaxed? Proponents of this method believe that it is extremely beneficial for those who are suffering from post-traumatic stress disorder (PTSD) and anxiety-related mental illnesses.

- Using breathing exercises to overcome fear

One of the major signs of a panic attack caused by fear is irregular breathing. Since fear makes us feel as if our chest is constricted, we try to increase our oxygen intake by taking rapid, shallow breaths. However, this causes a lesser amount of oxygen to be absorbed by the lungs, which in turn can affect the functioning of vital organs such as the heart and the brain. Therefore, you need to figure out a way to keep your breathing at a normal pace when you experience fear-related symptoms. Try this, take a deep breath now, and feel how that process refreshes your mind and body. Guided meditation and certain breathing exercises have been known to distract your brain from the fear-inducing stimuli and instead focus on your bodily functions—in this case, breathing.

- The Sedona Method

A lot of people choose to dismiss this particular strategy just because it's simple and easy. Don't be fooled by its directness. This is one of the most effective methods out there to let go of different feelings that end up becoming a barrier between you and your goals! All you have to do is ask yourself these three, fundamental questions while focusing on your fear and its emotional impact:

1. Could I let go of this feeling?
2. Would I let go of this feeling?
3. When will I let go of this feeling?

The first step is to acknowledge the depth of your fear and let it wash over yourself. In this way, you allow it to exit your subconscious, where it has been secretly manipulating your behaviors, and enter your conscious mind.

Once you've managed to bring this emotion to the surface, reaffirm that you have the ability to let go of your fear. Prepare your mind to detach it from your fear and move on to the second question.

Now ask yourself if you want to continue to distress your mind and heart by clinging to your fear or let it flow out of you so that you can escape its clutches.

Once you've completed the first two steps, you will feel your resistance slowly melting away because now you recognize the importance of unchaining yourself from the shackles of fear. It won't happen overnight, but if you make this a part of your daily routine, you'll find your fear evaporating into thin air with every passing day.

Everyday Strategies To Face Your Fears Your Fears

While these strategies can greatly reduce your sensitivity to fear and its overall influence on the mind and body, it's extremely important that you include certain habits within your lifestyle that can be used every day to combat this particular emotion. Here are three micro-habits that can transform your attitude and prepare you to be a fearless person that never stops chasing their passion.

- Try to be rejected more often

One way to get over your fear of rejection is through exposure; once you realize that the scenario you created in your mind is more intense and exaggerated as compared to reality, you'll find it much easier to build a resistance to this emotion. Try contacting strangers, famous people, or organizations that you'd love to collaborate with, even if you're sure that you'll receive no response. This will result in one of two outcomes; you might receive a response that accepts your request, or you might get one that denies it. Either way, you'll be contacted, and that is exactly what matters. When you do a cost-benefit analysis of this situation, you'll realize that there's nothing to lose but so much to gain! Spare two minutes from your day to make a phone call, which might alter your life forever! Even if you don't get the answers you're looking for, it will keep you motivated, and you will slowly overcome your fear of rejection.

- Positive affirmations

These optimistic statements aim to replace self-defeating thought patterns and negative thinking styles that entangle your mind in a complicated web of fear, self-loathing, and pessimism. Scientifically, positive affirmations not only serve as a reminder of what you want in your life and how you aim to pursue these goals but also help you adopt a thought pattern that is likely to attract success. Here is one affirmation that you can use in daily life:

I am prepared for X; I won't fail because I am ready to take on any challenges that come my way.

If you repeat this to yourself as soon as you wake up in the morning, you'll find a shift occurring in your outlook and approach towards life. We will deal with these statements in further detail in Chapter 8.

- Try to do one scary thing each day

Remember how we talked about the false security of comfort zones in the previous chapter? This habit will enable you to confront your fears head-on and prepare you to deal with a variety of challenges. The idea is to participate in things, activities, and events that scare you; constant exposure will desensitize you to the fear and prevent your body from going into a state of shock.

If you're terrified of public speaking, try to join the debate club at your college. It sounds counterintuitive, but there's a reason why this strategy is recommended by a lot of experts. It chips away at your fear until you realize that you are capable of achieving whatever you want.

Prepare for failure, but don't let it hold you down, especially when there's so much for you to explore and accomplish in life!

Chapter 4

How To Free Yourself From Distractions

Now that we've talked about fear and the strategies needed to conquer it. Let's discuss distractions.

Distractions seem to be what we like to be doing, but they don't align with our values, we just can't help doing it. For example, people are constantly distracted by their phones when they are doing things, and I believe nobody would put "scrolling the phone" as one of your desires since it doesn't fulfill you. Distractions keep us from accomplishing things we want to do.

The purpose of this chapter is to help you investigate the distractions that are holding you back from giving full attention to your passion. It will enable you to make a list of these factors by going through a series of rigorous questionnaires and tests, specifically designed to facilitate your understanding of yourself and your attachment to these distractions. Once you've accomplished this, you will find some techniques, tips, and methods on how to disconnect from distractors by not only removing them but also training your mind to resist falling back into old patterns.

But let's take this one step at a time.

So, how do we begin removing these elements from our environment?

I believe that the first step should be to identify the biggest distractors around you before you can implement any strategies to eliminate them. Like all exercises within this book, this one also begins with a little question and answer session. Think about the last time you found yourself swamped by distractions. Can you pinpoint what these were and how they affected your productivity? If you were distracted, how did you manage to get out of that rut?

The Three Biggest Distractions That Hold Us Back

The three universal distractors that afflict almost everyone, no matter what they do, are: clutter/Mental Clutter, social media/entertainment, and negative thought patterns. Let's take a look at how they impact your productivity and focus.

- Clutter/Mental Clutter

A lot of people underestimate the importance of working in a clutter-free environment. How many times have you worked in a disorganized and messy room? Were you able to get anything done without being distracted by the clutter around you? Physical clutter can overwhelm you and deceive you into believing that *nothing* is being done. You don't have to work in a spotlessly clean room, but it would certainly help relieve some stress if you remove anything that triggers your mind to lose focus on the task at hand. Remember all the times you tried to clean your room but were thrown off track by the discovery of some item that you had forgotten about? You find yourself reminiscing while clutching the object, having completely forgotten that you had initially set out to do something entirely different. The same principle applies to work in a cluttered environment; you will find yourself captivated with the most trivial of objects in an attempt to procrastinate and will not be able to accomplish your goals.

Let's talk about another kind of widely ignored disorganization– *mental clutter*.

So, what is mental clutter? It is a collection of sounds, images, ideas, and visual cues that overstimulate your brain and prevent you from focusing on an activity. Simply put, this kind of jumble refers to that overwhelming state of mind where you think that a lot of tasks are important and cannot focus due to the pressure. We've all had days where we felt so tired just thinking about all that needs to be done that we never managed to do anything at all. This is because we do not use our mind's organizational powers to the maximum and fail to categorize each task according to its difficulty level.

One way in which you can stop letting simple tasks eat up all your concentration is to take a calendar or a planner and make a list of all the things that need to be done in a single day. Then, decide which ones are more important than the others and require immediate attention, ranking each activity until you have sorted out the first task of the day. Start your day by accomplishing the easiest, least time-consuming ones; this little tip is immensely beneficial as the relief from finishing these activities gives your brain a boost, increases your enthusiasm, and puts you in a better, optimistic mood for the rest of the day.

- Social Media/Entertainment

We've all been victims of the social media loop. Any time our screens light up with a notification, we just *have* to go through every single app to check if we missed any important bit of news, messages, pictures, or comments. It's a vicious cycle that greatly decreases productivity levels and also contributes to our negative attitudes. Of course, we've all tried to deal with it by switching off our phones and disconnecting from the internet, but it's rarely an effective long-term solution.

Similarly, we've all been guilty of procrastinating on our work commitments by watching movies and shows on streaming services, listening to music, and generally filling up our time with other mindless bits of entertainment. It might seem harmless and fun, but the reality is that living in this distracted state greatly decreases our sensitivity to inspiration and passion.

One reason why I believe social media and entertainment to be particularly dangerous for a person who wants to live their best, passionate life is that it fills our mind with innutritious thoughts until we are consumed by negativity. Scrolling through Instagram, Facebook, Tik Tok, and Twitter all day can actually cause you to develop an inferiority complex; even if you're not actively aware of it, over time, you begin to compare yourself to everyone else and sink deeper into self-hatred. You feel as if you're the only one whose entire plan is falling apart when everyone else is enjoying their time and living a perfect life. Even though you try to tell yourself that not everything you see on social media reflects the truth, a tiny part of your mind continues to add negative thoughts that can overwhelm and discourage you from your mission. Furthermore, this is another way for negative people to gain access to you and bring you down with their constant criticisms. Their resentment and pessimism seep into your mind and fills it up with poisonous, self-defeating thoughts, which become a giant barrier in your quest for passion and fulfillment. One simple advice here is to deactivate the auto-login function, especially when you are working. You will have to remember your password and type them every time you want to log in, which will prevent you from habitually log in your social media accounts.

- Negative attitudes
    - Grudge

Believe it or not, maintaining grudges can actually sap the life out of you.

A lot of mental energy is wasted in thinking about the people who have wronged us in life. Instead of processing this hatred, we let it overwhelm our hearts and minds and carry them within us every single day. This emotional baggage disrupts your energy and takes up an enormous amount of space in your mind that should be filled by inner peace. Don't let yourself become a vessel for anyone's rage; instead of waiting for incomplete, meaningless apologies, take the high road, and exorcise these memories from your mind. Once you free yourself from nuisances, you allow your mind to open itself to positive feelings and experiences, which are essential for anyone who wants to live passionately. Try to think about all the ways these people changed your life for the better and the lessons they taught you, which helped your personal and emotional growth. Your appreciation to them will negate any toxic feelings that still might be bottled up inside of you.

o   Worrying

Don't make the mistake of undermining the role that worry plays in distracting you. Have you ever been so overwhelmed by worries that you felt like you were frozen in place, unable to do anything at all? Did you think of all the worst possible outcomes of a situation and failed to complete even the simplest of tasks? That's what worrying does to your mind. You imagine horrible things that bear no resemblance to reality; think of these thoughts as an alarm that constantly rings even if there's no danger in sight. It seems ridiculous to lose focus on something that doesn't even exist, but that's exactly how our mind tricks us into procrastinating on important activities. When you learn to silence this anxious, internal monologue, you will find yourself approaching each task with renewed vigor. One piece of advice to stop worry from consuming you is to take action. Let the action takes over your fear!

However, getting rid of these distractions isn't the full answer to your dilemma; the point is to flex the muscles in your mind and teach it to maintain an intense level of concentration that is unwavering even in the presence of these distractors; it sounds difficult, but once you begin incorporating these upcoming strategies in your daily routine you'll find that the answers have been staring you in the face this whole time.

Now that we've covered the three biggest distractions and their effects on your daily productivity, it is time to see what specifically is holding us back. We will begin by using the self-diagnostics approach; below are two checklists that have been designed to help you identify the thoughts and actions that are currently affecting your concentration and performance.

Identify What's Holding You Back

These self-diagnostic worksheets have been obtained from Living Life to the Full, a website dedicated to helping people become a better version of themselves by replacing negativity with health, peace, and passion. Place a tick against each thought and behavior that you can relate to and try to summarize what you've learned from each checklist.

- Checklist 1—What Do I Think That Is Holding Me Back?
  - ❏ Do you constantly criticize yourself?
  - ❏ Do you fixate on the negative side of a situation?
  - ❏ Are you pessimistic about the future and expecting everything to turn out badly?
  - ❏ Do you find yourself jumping to the worst conclusions?
  - ❏ Do you automatically assume that others view you in a bad way?
  - ❏ Do you find yourself taking responsibility for everything, even if it isn't your fault?
  - ❏ Do you always have unreasonable standards for yourself?

- Checklist 2—What Do I Do That Is Holding Me Back?
  - ❏ Are you eating too many sweet things?
  - ❏ Sitting around all day?
  - ❏ Spending too much or little?
  - ❏ Are you taking your prescribed medication regularly?

- ❑ Shutting down and repressing your anxieties/stress?
- ❑ Depending on others to help you?
- ❑ Lashing out at people?
- ❑ Trusting people you don't really know?
- ❑ Are you overdoing the phone calls?
- ❑ Hiding away?
- ❑ Being impulsive about important things?
- ❑ Setting yourself up to fail/be rejected?
- ❑ Becoming a TV/Internet addict?
- ❑ Relying on other people to fix all your problem?
- ❑ Constantly keeping yourself busy?
- ❑ Consuming an excess amount tea/coffee/alcohol to increase energy?
- ❑ Sleeping in the whole day?
- ❑ Putting things off?
- ❑ Worrying all the time?

You know you want to do better, but you don't know where to start. Or maybe you're afraid of change and don't know how you'll deal with an unfamiliar routine. By filling these worksheets, you will be able to identify the areas where you need to improve and change.

How To Eliminate The Non-essential

Regardless of where you stand right now, these strategies are small, almost unnoticeable changes that will give your brain an immense boost if you use them every day. The aim is to make these gradual modifications in your routine until they become a permanent part of your belief-system. Don't allow fear to dominate you, test each strategy for a week, and observe the difference; in this way, you can test which ones work best for you!

- The 'Close the Door' hack

One way in which you can eliminate these non-essential elements is to implement the Close The Door trick. Believe it or not, this simple trick takes less than ten seconds and stops you from procrastinating. Just get up and close the door to your bedroom or office! Trusted by successful professionals all over the world, this gets rid of unwanted distractions by removing them from the premises and letting everyone know that you are not to be disturbed. Just as you would close the door of your room to get some privacy and silence, let people know that you're busy with an important task so that you can dedicate all of your energy to finishing it. Once you start disconnecting from the chaos around you, you will find it fairly easy to focus on your goals.

- Limit scroll time

This Forbes approved method can do wonders for your concentration span!

It will be especially beneficial for those who find it hard to leave their phones and sit down to work. If you're plagued by the endless scrolling curse, I suggest that you begin by noting down the amount of time spent each day, going through social media apps. Now that you've identified the problem and its intensity, try gradually cutting down on this habit by limiting your scroll time. You don't have to completely disengage yourself by deleting them, I believe it's counterproductive, and you'll fall back into old habits in no time; what you need to do is slowly decrease the time you spend on these apps and restrict yourself from using them beyond the allotted time-frame. You can still enjoy yourself without being engulfed by the virtual world; take advantage of browser extensions and apps that prevent you from accessing these sites beyond a predetermined time limit. They also enable you to monitor your productivity and time spent on each activity so that you can make adjustments to your daily schedule.

- Be conscious of social media interactions

Sometimes social media can drain your energy for other reasons; maybe the problem isn't that you spend too much time on social media but the *interactions* that you have on these platforms. Maybe your Facebook friends are constantly bombarding you with their criticisms, infesting your mind with their negativity. Perhaps the content they share is triggering and sends you into a spiral of overthinking. Maybe you face bullying or harassment on these sites, which brings you down and transforms you into a self-deprecating, anxious person who is overwhelmed by these attitudes and feelings. In this case, the issue isn't your addiction to scrolling through social media; it's just that you're not connected to the right people. If used correctly and effectively, social media can be a great way to find and share your passion with other people; think about all the individuals who went from being dispassionate, unhappy workers trapped in the daily 9 to 5 routine to successful, happy, and fulfilled individuals who used their online presence to create and promote their personal brand. You can do that too! But you'll have to let go of any unhealthy interactions that can cause negative thoughts to accumulate in your mind. Make no mistake—toxicity is not the same as conflict. Avoiding toxicity means that you do not want pointless, unhealthy attitudes and behaviors to harm your mental health. On the other hand, conflict not only broadens your horizons but can actually contribute to your knowledge of the real world. It drives understanding, compassion, and helps you to see the world from a different, new perspective. Keeping this in mind, make sure that you engage with content that boosts your brain and expands your worldview.

- Balance social commitments

Similarly, your social commitments can also affect your productivity. While it's natural to spend time with your friends and family, it's essential that you maintain a balance between these engagements and your personal development. You cannot let your growth be affected by any distractions as it just drives you away from your real goal: finding your passion. Try to ensure that these social commitments do not interfere with the time that you've set aside for reflection and self-improvement; if you let them take over your entire schedule, you will find yourself constantly drained and tired. As we discussed before, taking time off can actually strengthen your relationship with friends and family, increasing the quality of time spent together as you are not constantly exhausted by their demands and really want to be around them. Practice saying no using the techniques mentioned in Chapter 2! The moment you turn your focus inward, you will discover the numerous advantages of prioritizing your personal needs over everyone and everything else.

- Create a 'Most Important Tasks' list

If you're distressed by the number of unfinished tasks piling up in your planner, and you're too frazzled to even sort out through the mess, then the Most Important Tasks method will be your new best friend. The idea behind this strategy is to eliminate, delegate, and simplify activities, chores, and duties that look complex and can be mentally exhausting to think about. Sit down with a notebook and pull up your calendar. Make a list of everything that needs to be done in a day and make a note of any deadlines that need to be met. You'll begin to observe that each task is different from the others in its difficulty level and the amount of time it takes to get done. Rank each task from the easiest to the most difficult and time-consuming. Often, a lot of small chores accumulate over time and trick your brain into thinking that you've got a lot to do. Group these together and set them aside for the time being. Now, return your attention to the big tasks and try to eliminate the ones which seem unnecessary and do not add to your happiness and fulfillment. It might seem like you're being selfish, but the truth is that you need to learn how to say no to things that become a burden on your schedule. Try narrowing the list until you're down to three, absolutely essential tasks per day. When you're done, schedule a time-frame for each task. In this way, you're imposing deadlines on yourself and sending signals to your mind to switch into productivity mode. The small set of easy tasks can be done in between the breaks you'll take after the completion of each major activity.

Reward yourself after completing each milestone so that you can condition your brain into maintaining a similar routine and work-ethic in the future. In this small, simple way, you not only learn to declutter your mind until the to-do list doesn't appear so daunting but also inculcate the amount of discipline needed to progress in your professional life.

Let's talk about the big changes that you can make in your daily life to improve concentration and focus. You've learned a lot about the small things that can help remove distractions from your immediate surroundings, but a big part of finding your passion is exercising self-restraint and training your mind to move past these distractions and focus on the big picture—your dreams and goals.

Everyday Exercises To Build Focus

- Use the Pomodoro Method

The Pomodoro Method is just one example of a strategy that can greatly increase your focus and productivity. It's recommended by a lot of experts since it aligns with the findings collected from different research studies that have observed and analyzed the function and capacity of the human brain. Think of it as a fun game; all you have to do is select a task, set a time limit for it, and try to complete it within this deadline. It is advised that you build up your concentration span by beginning from 25 minutes and increasing your way up to 45 minutes, in a week's duration. Every time your alarm rings to notify you that the time is up, indulge in a ten or fifteen-minute break and catch up with your friends, listen to music, or eat something you like.

Once your little break is over, try to return to your desk to finish a different task. In this way, you're exercising the muscles in your brain through conditioning and giving yourself time to relax once you've accomplished your goal. Using this strategy can change the way you approach work; it will help you realize that setting these small time-limits can actually declutter your mind and prevent you from feeling overwhelmed. The inclusion of breaks leaves you with enough time to unwind until it's time to get back to work again! Try it out for an entire week and test its efficacy yourself!

- Dedicate time to learning every day

Ever wondered how successful people are able to acquire knowledge about global issues while maintaining excellence in their professional careers?

The solution is astounding in its simplicity. They set aside time to learn new things *every single day.*

A lot of people doubt this strategy—they don't understand how learning fits into the great scheme of finding their passion. But when you really think about it, maybe one reason why you haven't found your passion is that you don't know it exists. Or you don't know anything about it. So far, we've come to understand that being good at something, a particular subject, a skill, or a field doesn't necessarily mean that it has to be your passion. So maybe—and hear me out—you haven't found your calling because your knowledge of the world is limited to events that take place in your immediate environment. People who are passionate about their profession invest a considerable amount of time in learning about the world beyond their ecosystem and, therefore, have a lot of knowledge about the emerging fields that are expanding our understanding of the universe and its inhabitants.

You can readily recognize a person who is dedicated to learning new things each day. They have a remarkably strong concentration span, acquired from hours of dedicated reading, and have maximized their brain's power to retain information. As a result, they have an expansive memory, formed through years of learning new bits of knowledge. These people do not subscribe to myopic world-views; their strength lies in their ability to examine an issue from all angles, even if they have not experienced it first-hand. Consequently, they are more empathetic than the average person and, therefore, more committed to being responsible community members. It is also unsurprising that these individuals are reflective, analytic, and have superb written and verbal communication skills. This is because learning teaches you to explore dimensions without being held back by your opinions or beliefs. It demands that you remain neutral and unbiased while assessing an issue so that your analysis is based on reason and logic, rather than uninformed opinions. Prolonged exposure to well-written fiction and non-fiction books also enhances your vocabulary and adds clarity to self-expression.

Take the example of two well-known people; actress, media executive, philanthropist Oprah Winfrey, and business magnate Bill Gates, the co-founder of the Microsoft Corporation. The latter has often talked about the importance of reading in his life and claims to read fifty books a year, which means that he goes through a new book each week. Similarly, Winfrey hosts a monthly book club meeting, where she selects a new text to be discussed by the members for each session. This indicates the sheer importance of reading in daily life. It doesn't matter what you read; it can be fiction, non-fiction, or even a newspaper! What matters is that you keep your brain engaged with productive, valuable exercises that will revolutionize your personality and professional life.

- Use podcasts and audiobooks

A lot of people struggle with reading and think that there's no way for them to add to their knowledge. A huge benefit of technological advancements is that there are more ways to learn now than ever before! Don't like reading? Listen to an audiobook instead! If that still doesn't work for you, switch to podcasts! They represent the perfect balance between fun and information. You can learn even when you're on the go; just plug in your earphones and absorb new knowledge while you go about your day.

- Virtual classes

Want to learn a new skill? Take virtual classes and courses designed to help you master any field of your choosing. The point is to commit to learning and find out what works best for you. We've entered a new, advanced digital age where anything is possible if you concentrate. Don't let these learning opportunities slip by; you might just discover fascinating things about yourself and your passion.

It's difficult to change, but nothing worthwhile ever happens if you stay stuck in the same, monotonous, toxic routine. Trust yourself—you can do great things if you stop letting distractions rule your life.

Chapter 5

Listen To Your Heart And Not Your Head

Now that we've learned the strategies needed to deal with distractions and improve focus. Let's take another step forward in creating a plan to find your true passion in life!

Aristotle, the ancient Greek philosopher, believed that the only difference between humans and other living species was the former's ability to think rationally.

Perhaps this is why humans are so obsessed with reason and logic; we think that the success of any venture depends on whether all decisions were grounded firmly in rationality.

People like scientists, stock market traders, engineers, doctors, etc. were educated to make decisions based on reality and rationality. However, when it comes to finding your passion, your rationality does not work that well since your passion is something linked to your soul. The heart tells you the voice of your spirit, your deep feelings. It is the feeling that when you think about something, your heart starts to beat fast. Feel that beat, instead of analyzing with your brain. Your brain brings you the voice of your rationality while your heart brings you the voice of your soul.

It's Scientifically Proven That You Should Do What You Love And Not What You Think Is Logical!

You might be wondering why it's so important to consult the heart in purely practical matters. If facts weren't enough to convince you, let's take a look at how this can benefit your lifestyle in visible ways.

- Reduces anxiety and stress

Imagine a world where you were able to do whatever you *really* wanted. You would be free; not bound by the shackles of logic or duty. No sneaky, self-defeating whispers of doubt would exist to constantly make you feel guilty for choosing your passion over everything else. In this parallel universe, you would be a better person, more in control of your emotions, empathetic, energetic, and definitely happier. The truth is that you can create this reality for yourself, even right now. If you quiet down and let your heart do the talking, you'll realize that this inner voice isn't as detached from reason as we are taught to believe. It actually shows you the path to contentment and satisfaction, which appears daunting and indomitable because *you* do not allow yourself to dream big. Listen to your heart and consult it during important decisions, and you will find yourself less anxious and stressed because you are not being bogged down by expectations.

- Allows you to experience healthier relationships

People who allow their heart to communicate with them are also able to maintain better relationships because they do not allow logic to confuse them; their empathy for other people makes them a better listener and a reliable individual. Instead of functioning according to rigid rules, they step outside the box and focus on the greater good, while also working on personal growth. This self-awareness also enables them to prioritize their happiness, which means that they are not constantly stressed out or overwhelmed. Such an outlook on life results in a healthy, balanced, and realistic personality, which is essential for positive relationships.

- Helps you succeed in the workplace

Contrary to popular belief, these individuals are not emotional, volatile, and high-strung. Since they're in contact with their authentic self, they are able to introspect and reflect on their actions and attitudes. This gives their intelligence an analytic as well as a holistic edge; due to these qualities, they are able to easily navigate the complexities in their professional life and make for better employees. Their success in the workplace stems from their ability to adjust, adapt, mediate, and empathize with other people; since they refuse to be led by the *shoulds* of society, their work reflects passion and enthusiasm for what they do.

Think about your previous paradigms; do you still believe that people who listen to their hearts are irrational, or do you now see the value of trusting your intuition? Finding your passion isn't possible if you just use your brain but not your heart. Sooner or later, you'll just find yourself in another dead-end, disheartened to your core because your approach was flawed in its essence.

When you're just starting out in your journey to reach your authentic self and have no idea of how to get your heart to take the steering wheel again, you might feel as if you will never be able to silence your doubts.

Everything seems blurred, confusing, and difficult. It seems as if you'll always have to live by the rules and can never escape the prison that your mind has created. It's natural to despair and find yourself lost. It's also normal to fear big changes. However, you don't have to start by turning your life upside-down. In the following section, we will discuss a number of different exercises that you can gradually introduce in your routine to practice the art of listening.

Everyday Exercises To Start Listening To Your Heart

- Don't trust your bad moods

The first tip is relatively simple. Don't try to talk to yourself when you're in a bad mood. In this state, everything appears black and white. You jump to conclusions and accept baseless beliefs into your system. A bad mood exaggerates the worst parts of reality and makes you feel as if there is nothing you can do to change. You sink into self-pity, use harsh labels for yourself, and constantly reprimand your mind and heart for leading you astray. Wait until you feel these self-defeating thoughts slip away. Clarity can never be found in clutter; the best thing you can do is to let go of the negativity and get into a clear headspace. Trying to communicate with yourself when you're not ready to face reality actually drones out your inner voice, rendering the entire exercise null and void. Once you have achieved a calmer state of mind, sit down and try to listen to what your heart says.

Take my word for it; the voice will be so much louder and clearer than before.

- Explore nature to get in touch with your authentic self

Cityscapes can sometimes add to a sense of doom and misery; even though they are extremely functional in their design, a change of environment can actually help you to get in touch with your heart. Looking at the same building every day can instill a sense of monotony, which compels you to resist change. One of the easiest ways that you can refresh your mind and heart is to find an escape in nature. Go for a short walk in the park or choose a hiking trail; it's completely up to you! Just make sure that you're alone with your thoughts and away from the noise. Being out in nature can remove the burden that negative thoughts constantly assert on our mind and can bring inner peace and harmony. Get some fresh air, and you'll find yourself closer to the ultimate prize: your heart's voice.

No Passion Or Too Many Passions To Focus On?

- Journal as much as you can!

I've emphasized the importance of writing stuff down to untangle emotions and declutter the mind. Journaling is perhaps the best way to escape from the real world and find yourself. It is especially beneficial because you're not being judged by anyone and can write down whatever you feel without fearing censure or disapproval. Think of your journal as a friend that just wants to listen to you and not give any advice at all. The objective is not to write positive things and then force yourself to feel something; all you have to do is write down what comes to your mind when you think about your passion. What were your hopes and dreams as a child before the weight of expectations crushed you? What do you yearn for in life? Remember, there are no wrong answers at all. Whatever you jot down is just there to help you navigate the complexities of life.

- Dedicate some time to meditation

You must be familiar with the concept of meditation and how it reduces stress, anxiety, and gives you time to introspect on your thoughts and actions. Deep breathing is one form of meditation that can help you stay grounded in reality and focus on the present. Apart from its numerous benefits for mental health, this exercise can actually help release up to seventy percent of the toxins that accumulate in your body throughout the day.

Sparing even ten minutes each day and spending that time engaging in daily guided meditations can instill mindfulness, changing the way you perceive the world and process your emotions.

- Practice silence

Disconnect from the noise around you, and I mean this in both a literal and metaphorical sense. It isn't just keeping quiet and isolating yourself; this is an exercise in mindfulness and refers to a headspace where you can introspect. Don't just disconnect from the noise around you, try to quieten the nagging voice inside your head, which traps your mind into a loop of anxiety and stress. Silence allows you to confront yourself and reflect on how you can do better. Try to practice this each day until you come to appreciate its impact on your daily routine.

- Find your mantra

This strategy is somewhat similar to the positive affirmations that we discussed in Chapter 3. Your task is to pick a statement that rejuvenates your soul and puts you in an optimistic state of mind so that you can go out into the world with positive energy radiating from your body. Repeat the same sentence to yourself each day; it doesn't have to be complex, stick to phrases that remind you to live fully in the present.

- Physical exercises in listening to your heart

We talked about the connection between physical and mental health in Chapter 1; another way that you can train yourself to listen to your heart is through physical exercise. This activity releases a combination of neurotransmitters and hormones that increase overall happiness and productivity. Your task is to figure out an exercise regimen that can easily fit into your daily routine and suits your body type. Build your stamina by starting from cardio, such as running or jogging, and then move to more advanced exercises.

Now that we've discussed different kinds of exercises that can guide you towards a more introspective approach. Let's take a look at two strategies that you need to commit to, starting today!

Strategies To Commit To Listening To Your Heart

- The 5 Second rule

Ever had a great idea but couldn't muster the energy to execute it because your brain started to interfere? According to Mel Robbins, author of *The 5 Second Rule,* this happens because your mind tries to make you procrastinate by providing you with multiple reasons for abandoning your idea, all of which appear logical. To truly break free from this habit, begin to take action within five seconds!

- Commit and report your progress publicly

If you commit to your goals publicly and try to report your progress to public platforms, you are more likely to stick to your target! There are two reasons why this system works for a lot of people. Firstly, the encouragement you receive from your audience fuels your enthusiasm and increases your confidence in yourself. Secondly, it creates accountability; if you do not declare your goals publicly, it's easy to lose interest in attaining them as time goes by because the only person who knows and cares is you. However, other people are likely to inquire about your progress, which motivates you to keep going until you reach the finish line.

The same principle underlies the idea of having a goal buddy. Get a friend or family member to start this journey with you so that you can both support, encourage, and check-in with each other to prevent losing sight of what you set out to achieve!

Chapter 6

Define Your Passion In 10 Questions

So far in this book, we have identified our desire, rated our values, figured out what we don't want in our life, fought our deepest fears, removed our distractions, and learned to pay attention to the voice of our soul rather than making all our decisions based on reason and logic. You are now fully prepared to search for your life's passion.

But what if I were to tell you that everything you've ever known about passion is fundamentally *wrong*?

You might disagree; after all, it's impossible to *not* know what passion means—you've spent a lot of time thinking about it, you're surrounded by people who swear that they've discovered its essence and are currently living their best life. You might even scoff and think about how absurd the statement sounds, considering that you're bombarded by evidence on a daily basis.

Let's begin by going back in time for a little exercise.

When was the first time you heard the word passion being used? Search your memory and try to recall the earliest instance at which the word became a part of your daily vocabulary. At this point, most of you will realize that you've heard it countless times as a child, ever since you began to use words to interact with the world. The question remains—*do you know what passion is?* Can you describe the emotional, mental, and cognitive states involved, are you able to accurately identify it, is your understanding of the concept realistic, and do you know the most efficient way to pursue it?

You might feel confident right now because you think you have the answers to all these questions; it is a flash of inspiration that hits all of a sudden and manages to change the course of your life forever. *Wrong.*

Here's the honest truth—these generally accepted ideas about passion, which are etched into our minds from a young age, are so removed from reality that they not only prevent you from being honest with yourself but also hold you back from putting in the mental energy needed to get in touch with your authentic self. A lot of people told you to chase your dreams and only pursue opportunities that align with your passions; you've heard it everywhere, but no one prepares you for the confusion, exhaustion, and soul-searching that is needed to reach this stage. No one tells you that it's not always like a bolt of lightning or a revelation; that sometimes, it takes a lot of thinking, questioning, and doubting to arrive at any concrete conclusions. Pop culture and media drill the exact same idea into your head by constantly presenting you with the stories of different individuals who achieved fame, wealth, and satisfaction, claiming that it was only possible because they were passionate about their work and whole-heartedly believed in it. They make it seem effortless and glamorous; this romanticized portrayal of the journey from realization to achievement makes you believe that success will just arrive at your doorstep once you become consciously aware of the profession that you want to invest your time and energy in.

Even the idea of it is diluted with conventionality; if your passion does not fit within the narrow, suffocating confines of what is acceptable in society, it is dismissed by everyone around you.

The truth stands in stark contrast to this depiction; finding your passion isn't the end of the road; it is the foundation on which you are supposed to build your life. All of this takes curiosity, resilience, discipline, and an ability to be brutally honest with yourself. If you're prepared to detach yourself from these unrealistic ideas about passion and get right to work, you will not only be able to achieve your goals but will also manage to acquire the various skills that are common among all highly effective individuals.

What Passion Is And Isn't

So here's what passion absolutely isn't.

- It is not burning desire

There's a fine line between desire, impulse, and passion. It may seem blurred to you right now, but as you answer the questions in this chapter, you'll begin to understand that there's a huge difference; desire is like the flame of a burning candle. You're immensely attracted to it in the beginning. It seems like the solution to all your problems.

It shines bright and bold, but sooner or later, the candle melts, and the flame goes out.

Passion *cannot* be extinguished.

It never wavers. It is solid, staunch, and gives you invaluable happiness.

It is independent of all concepts of time.

- It is not a weekend activity

You might have a ton of hobbies that you enjoy doing in your free time, but that doesn't make them your *true* passion.

It's particularly interesting when I ask people to describe their passion, and they begin by listing their weekend activities. While some people do find their life's calling in their hobbies, the two don't have to coincide each time. Maybe you enjoy painting and are extremely skilled at it, but you don't seem to find the fulfillment that successful individuals talk about.

- It is not an urge

Don't settle for what you think you should like. Keep searching, asking questions, crossing out what doesn't sit right with you. Continue indulging in your hobbies, but don't delude yourself into thinking that something is your passion just because you like doing it on the weekends. This goes beyond the simplicity of *like*. Passion is doing something that you *love* and can't imagine a life without.

Now that we have a fair understanding of what passion isn't. Let's take a look at what it really means.

- Passion is a strong sense of *why*.

It gives meaning to your life and is a strong part of your sense of self. It makes you want to get up each day and conquer the world. It's not a trifling desire or an enjoyable activity. It's the legacy you want to leave behind.

- It is something that you can be proud of.

Everyone wants to leave their mark on the world. They want to leave this world, draped in glory and fame. Your passion is something that you want others to remember you by even after you're long gone.

Now begins the hard part.

In all my years as a career coach, I've encountered numerous people who find themselves adrift in life and need help to reconnect with the innovative part of their authentic selves. In order to help them form a solid image of their vision, I've crafted ten questions that are sure to facilitate the average person in figuring out their mission in life. The only thing that I require from you during this exercise is a strong commitment to truth.

Leave your expectations outside the door. Silence any whispers of doubt and hate that have haunted you ever since you set out on this journey. It's time that you get in touch with what you really, *truly* want.

The Questions

- What did you want to be when you grew up?

Children have this remarkable gift for following their hearts' desires and resisting the weight of expectations. They use their youth, creativity, and imagination to the fullest. Think about your passion as a child; were you specifically interested in certain fields, objects, and topics? Did you want to pursue a particular career option but were talked out of it by your parents and teachers? The purpose of going down memory lane is to understand how your mind worked in that autonomous, energetic phase of life. Maybe you've outgrown your childhood passion and want something different. Just write it down and think about the aspects of this profession that excited you. What we're looking for here is simple; you want to think about the features of your ideal career. Figuring out your passion is about finding things in common with what you wanted as a child when you weren't burdened by hundreds of negative narratives.

- What about you today would make your eight-year-old self cry?

Don't let go of that thread, which connects you to your inner child just yet!

Reflect on how you've changed over time. What qualities and attributes did you possess as a child that is now buried under the rubble? Have you gained any traits that would upset your younger self? Can you detect any damaging, hurtful thought patterns? Maybe you were immensely fascinated by robots as an eight-year-old and used to imagine that they were alive and could move at your command. Now you might be a salesperson in an insurance company who has lost that passion and interest. Would your younger self cry at this? Would they be upset that you lost your way in life and don't do the one thing that used to make you alive? This question helps you unlearn the toxicity that you have been injected with as you grew up. It is meant to uncover the real *you*, the self that existed before it was hammered into someone else's version of acceptable. Make a note of all the aspects of yourself and circumstances that would distress the eight-year-old you. These lists will help you formulate a map and add strategies that can effectively deal with each component that you want to modify.

- Do items on your shopping list share any common features?

What do you spend money on?

Skim through the recent items you've bought with your credit card. Do you notice any recurring purchases? Do any of these have similar traits, uses, and attributes? Another way to understand your tastes and look for passion in what you enjoy consuming is to look at your movie and book collections. What topics, themes, and genres do you find entertaining? Try to ground your happiness for solid reasons; for example, if you enjoy reading about psychology and recent developments in the field, you can trace your liking back to a deep interest in the mind and behavior of human beings. With this little exercise, you can discover what truly moves your soul and challenges your mind.

- Is there something you can't stop talking about with the people around you?

Maybe it's an idea that you have never considered as your passion before because it seems unrealistic and difficult to accomplish. Or you just haven't been able to hear your inner voice over the din.

One reason why people often end up ignoring this vital sign is that they do not make the connection between passion and excitement.

In your head, passion looks profitable and logical. You know you'll have to work hard, but the idea that you could actually enjoy your work seems too good to be true. If this resonates with you, then you're halfway there! Ask your family, colleagues, and even your friends if they can point out a particular topic that you're thrilled to discuss at all times. Anything that exhilarates you and propels you to action is your passion.

- What new things are you dying to try out?

Sometimes your passion is right in front of you, staring you right in the eye, but you can't seem to recognize it because you're trained to ignore your heart. Have you formed an interest in attaining any skills? What aspects of these activities excite you? If you methodically question yourself, you'll find that the answers are obvious and simple. One of my friends found his passion in the same way! He started brewing in his garage just because he couldn't help trying that out, and now he owns a large brewery with hundreds of employees. Don't wait for opportunities to walk to you. It doesn't work like that! Stay on the lookout for activities that might expand your horizons. Go out, engage with the world, and constantly think of new ways in which you can push yourself to do better.

- What makes you forget to eat?

Passion isn't a tepid attachment to a goal. It's all-consuming, taking over your senses and your brain till you cannot rest until you've pushed it out of your system, into existence. Have you ever been engaged in doing something that you forget to eat? Search hard; that is where your passion lies. Nothing seems to deter you from your path; hunger, pain, sleep, and rest become unimportant, even non-essential. It's as if the world revolves around you and your passion; everything else is secondary. A lot of people find this description ludicrous, but it's not just a string of convincing words made to deceive you into being unrealistic. This is exactly how successful, passionate people like Steve Jobs, Walt Disney, Stephen King, Oprah Winfrey, and Bill Gates feel every day of their lives. It isn't because they're inherently different from you; it's because they refused to settle for any less, and you can do the same. Your passion is supposed to hijack every part of your body. It controls you until every action stems from pure inspiration and glory, not logic and reason. This is what you should aim for. Your dream life is just waiting to be manifested.

- How can you better embarrass yourself?

It's human nature to want to look like you've got it all together.

But have you ever tried to actively embarrass yourself in front of other people?

It might seem like a ridiculous idea, but here's a thought; remember how you stopped yourself from asking questions in class because you were too afraid of looking stupid in front of other people?

It might seem insignificant to you, but in this struggle to appear knowledgeable, you actually end up losing on opportunities to learn and grow.

You might be made to feel like you're dumb for raising your voice.

People might jeer and laugh at you, but what would you prefer: to look stupid for five minutes in front of people whose opinions are not going to matter in the grand scheme of things or to remain ignorant for the rest of your life.

Don't let your fear of being embarrassed ever stop you from learning. Think about Michael Jordan, who was told that he was too short to play when he first applied to be in his high school basketball team. He offered to clean the floor after each training, and in that way, he was accepted. Nobody knew that he would go on to become one of the greatest basketball players of all time! He could've let the comments hold him back, but he didn't accept any excuses and kept moving forward.

So ask yourself this: how can you better embarrass yourself? What opportunities have you been neglecting simply because you're too conscious of other people's opinions? In this realm of honesty and openness, you'll finally find your lost, wandering spirit.

- What would you do for a year if you only had a year to live?

When you imagine the future, do you see an endless string of black and white days, stretching into infinity, spent in misery and unhappiness? Or are you procrastinating on finding your purpose simply because you think you have all the time in the world? Often, people find themselves paralyzed into inactivity simply because they think they have their whole lives ahead of them to explore their passion.

The truth couldn't be more different: we don't know what the future will hold. We barely even know if we'll make it through the next day.

What if you weren't held down by time and existence? Think about all the projects you would pursue if you knew that your time on earth was limited to 365 days. Make a list of all these activities and think of it as a type of bucket list. This question will help you prioritize your desires and reframe your needs, allowing you to focus on what really requires your attention.

- What would you do if you knew you couldn't fail?

We've talked about the dangers of being controlled by fear in Chapter 3. But what if this fear of failure didn't exist? What goals would you pursue if you weren't being held back by these mental barriers? When you remove the failure factor from the equation, you begin to form certain ideas about what you really desire from your professional life. Instead of thinking in black and white terms, try to envision a life where you were bound to succeed. The clarity you will gain from this visualization exercise will finally reveal all the goals that you want to pursue in this lifetime.

- If you had 5 minutes and the whole world was forced to listen, what would you say?

Think of the entire world as your stage. Let's set up the clock now, and your five minutes start once you hear the click. Now imagine the clock clicked, and everyone in the world was listening to you. What do you want to say to them? Prepare all the things you want to share with the world. It might be a promise, a secret, a plan, or a specific insight of the universe. Get your speech drafted, and you will find your passion in it.

With these questions, you can refine the concept of what passion means to you and create a plan that includes all the steps you need to take towards your ideal life. Just listen to your heart; the truth has always existed inside of you; just let it set you free!

Chapter 7

Too Many Passions? Which Is Profitable?

Are you the kind of person who roams around a gift shop for hours on end, unable to pick a present for your friend's birthday because you just can't decide which one would be the best? The colors swim at the corner of your eyes, hurting your head, launching a discordant chorus of questions until your mind is nothing but an echo chamber.

Have you ever been to a restaurant and just couldn't decide what type of iced-tea to order? It's not that you're a picky eater, you love all the flavors equally and can't pick which one you want to drink today. You analyze each option in terms of flavor, quality, quantity, color, but the thought of ordering the *wrong* drink upsets you so much that you end up ordering a coffee, foregoing iced-tea altogether.

Maybe you've got to decide what major to pursue in college. You know you want to study English Literature, but you're scared that it will eliminate any prospect of a profitable career, so you take up Psychology and History too, just to be safe. Everyone tells you to narrow it down and let go of the extraneous subjects, but you're frozen by a fear of regret, an outcome that doesn't even exist just yet. Consequently, by the time you begin to realize that studying three subjects at this level is exhausting and impractical, you have already wasted a lot of your time and energy. And you will have to go back to choose the one you need to stick to anyway.

Do you find yourself frustrated with the endless possibilities, constantly evaluating each option in your head, worried that you might end up skipping over the perfect opportunity? You might want to be a lawyer because it is cool and lucrative, but your lawyer friend tells you that it will be a path filled with learning boring terms and complex logic. Now you have heard people who had an MBA are living their dream life, and you might want to try that too. Your friend in the business school tells you that in order to succeed in the business world, you need to develop your network consistently, which requires frequently socializing with people, and that is not what you want. Then, you thought that you might be the next Steve Jobs and wanted to learn some computer techniques. In the end, you will find yourself staying at the same place, wasting all the time to decide which way to go. It's not that you're an indecisive person, it's just that you're so caught up in what-ifs that you end up not making a decision at all. The exhaustion of choosing between equally acceptable options sends your mind into a downward spiral of doubt and

If you've ever been in similar situations and reacted in the same way, even though all your options were perfectly acceptable, you, my friend, are plagued by a condition called FOBO.

What Is Fear Of Better Options (FOBO) And How To Get Over It?

You've undoubtedly heard of its equally annoying relative FOMO— 'fear of missing out'. Both terms were coined by venture capitalist Patrick McGinnis who described FOBO or 'fear of better options' as a psychosociological phenomenon where a person is paralyzed by indecision when confronted with multiple, equally suitable options. This fear isn't limited to big career decisions; it can disrupt your ability to make even the smallest of decisions such as choosing what to eat, wear, watch, drink, read, do, etc. It is also known as analysis paralysis, owing to the state of inactivity it induces in a person who is faced with any kind of decision-making.

McGinnis believes that this kind of fear has existed ever since the first humans began to walk on this planet. "These feelings are biologically part of who we are. I call it the biology of wanting the best," he asserts in an interview with *The New York Times*, "our ancestors a million years ago were programmed to wait for the best because it meant they were more likely to succeed" (Herrera, 2018). However, in this digital age, where technological advancements continue to dazzle the masses, FOBO is exacerbated by social media, which has opened up multiple avenues. We spend all day on our screens, comparing ourselves to people, and become overwhelmed by the variety of options at our disposal. Think about your online shopping habits: how many times did you end up not buying anything at all because you felt as if you should wait for a better option to show up before you made a purchase? As a result, you keep looking for an outcome that doesn't even exist when there is a plethora of existing, suitable options just waiting to be picked.

While FOBO has been linked to anxiety, psychologists remain unconvinced that this fear is its own category of anxiety disorder. "It is possible for anxiety to be experienced around many different issues, of which fear of choosing the wrong option in regards to big life decisions may be one," the chief executive of Anxiety UK, Nicky Lidbetter claims in an article published in *The Guardian*. "Fear of a better option, however, is more likely to be linked to or a trigger for a pre-existing anxiety condition as opposed to being sufficient to warrant being categorized as an anxiety disorder in its own right" (Khan, 2019).

How Is FOBO Connected To Passion?

In essence, FOBO is the fear that letting go of a certain option will cause regret later in life. You're held back by thoughts of a future where you wish that you hadn't dismissed any option at all. Obviously, you know that it's not realistic or practical to *never* choose a path just because you're scared of making the wrong decision or facing negative outcomes, but you find yourself making the same error over and over again. So maybe you have multiple ideas of what your passion should be, but you can't seem to choose one because you're afraid that you might end up picking the wrong one and will never get to reach your full potential.

No matter how you try to convince yourself that these thoughts are irrational, you find yourself in the same trap, spinning like a hamster on a wheel. Unproductive and exhausted.

You're no different than a hoarder who doesn't see the point of parting with objects, even if they're dusty, broken, and useless clutching on to every single option, afraid of eliminating any possibilities lest they turn out to be your life's calling.

Narrow Down Your Passions Through Questions

Asking yourself these four questions will help you translate your skills, wants, and motivations into a profitable passion. Remember to answer these questions from your own perspective instead of what others think about you; the whole objective of this exercise is to determine what's right for you, even if it might not fit within someone else's definition of passion.

- Is there anything you love doing that you're both knowledgeable about and good at?

It is not enough for a passion to be something that you're an expert in, a lot of experts often end up changing professional direction overnight simply because they do not enjoy their career even if they excel in it. Brilliance is never the sole indicator for fulfillment. People like Kobe Bryant, J.K. Rowling, Will Smith, and Taylor Swift found that one thing in which they excelled and made it their life's passion. Finding that intersection between expertise, motivation, and knowledge can be hard, I know, but unless you stop thinking of your life's calling as one-dimensional, you'll never be able to find a path that resonates with every fiber of your being.

- Do you have two or more passions in mind that you can integrate together?

For J.K. Rowling, author of the best-selling fantasy series, Harry Potter, inspiration struck when her admission applications were rejected by all the colleges she had applied to. It was a hard pill to swallow, but she soon realized that it had never really been her dream to study English Literature anyways. She narrowed down her interest to two fields that seemed to speak to her: psychology and writing. It began to dawn on her that she could amalgamate both of these passions into creating a fictional world and becoming a novelist.

Think about this strategy for a second. Rowling was able to recognize that she could use her fascination for psychology to write complex characters. Do you have any passions that can be formed into one cohesive career path? If so, can you list these and try to find the similarities between them? If you love video games and computer programming, why don't you write a video game yourself? If you love traveling and writing, why don't you start writing blogs or books about traveling? Once you try to shift focus from finding one goal to creating something from the talents and skills you already possess, you will begin to arrive at fascinating and viable conclusions about what you want to do for the rest of your life.

- What are you good at that you won't mind working at and/or learning more about?

It's perfectly normal if you feel as if you're not exactly an expert at your passion. As we've already discussed before, you don't have to be good at something for that particular area to be your passion. There's always room to acquire more knowledge and experience with time. However, sometimes when we begin to delve deeper into our supposed passion, we realize that the learning process isn't exactly enjoyable. It doesn't motivate you to take your skills to the next step; instead, it feels like a chore. As if you're pushing your body against natural forces, to do something that it's not exactly excited about.

Don't be alarmed! That's just your heart trying to guide you to an alternate path.

Learning more about your passion should never feel like a burden or a duty. The eagerness to acquire further knowledge should emanate from inside of your soul.

Let's say that you're good at drawing, but don't feel like you're an expert just yet; would you *want* to take drawing lessons to take your skills to the next level, or would you rather spend that time learning about something else? The idea is to think of something that you would happily want to learn about and pursue, even if your work isn't perfect.

Everyone wants their passion to yield profit. After all, it's natural to assume that success should be the next step once you connect to your true self and begin pursuing your dream.

But before you can jump into it, you need to do some preliminary research. Without an understanding of the risks and benefits involved, you might find yourself chasing a mirage. An easy way of narrowing down your passions to choose the most lucrative one is to use the internet to your advantage and analyze whether the public will be receptive to your ideas.

Use The Internet To Narrow Down Your Passions

- Is it a 'passion' or 'problem' business?

The first step is to identify whether your idea fits into a 'passion' or 'problem' category

There are two main motivators to every Google search; either you're exploring a subject that you're interested in or you're trying to purchase something. This is the passion versus problem divide that you need to have a thorough understanding of. Is your idea going to help people who are searching the internet for hobbies, entertainment, and other fun-related activities, or does it cater to people who are looking for solutions to their problems? Frequently, the two categories will overlap, and that's great! Your job is to take each item on the list that you created in the previous section and think about which groups it fits into. Use the six tools, websites, and techniques to further narrow down your niche and understand how your idea and audience are likely to interact with each other.

- Use *Answer the Public* to find more information about people's preferences and needs

This is an online, free keyword tool designed to help you figure out what your audience wants to know more about. It generates keyword searches within a particular field, helping you to understand whether their needs are passion or problem-oriented.

- Try *Google Keyword Planner* to find out what people need and love

All you have to do is type some keywords relevant to your idea, and this tool will generate an output in the form of phrases and terms. Your task is to filter through the output by adjusting the search volume, competition, and suggested bid. For monthly search volume, stay within the 1k-10k range. This is because a lower range indicates a smaller, less-desired market, which means that profitability will also be low. Similarly, for competition, choose the low-medium option—this should give you an estimate of the level of competition that currently exists. When looking at suggested bids, keep in mind that higher bids are related to high buyer intent. In this simple way, you can evaluate commercial intent and determine whether your idea is viable or not.

- Go through *Redditlist* to refine your niche

This is another option to investigate the interests of people all over the world. All you have to do is put in certain keywords related to your passion and surf through the different subreddits until you're able to define your business idea. In your search, you will come across various questions and themes that people are eager to talk about, which will further enable you to formulate a concrete plan.

- Use *Amazon* to investigate consumer behavior and see what people are buying

It's highly likely that you've used Amazon to make various online purchases in the past, but did you know that you could use it to do some research for your own product? Since it delivers nearly every product that could possibly exist, it's fairly easy to check whether your idea will be profitable by looking at the search results. Just type in the product that you have in mind and take a look at the number of results that pop up. Take it one step further and scroll through similar products to see whether these are popular and being regularly purchased by a lot of people. A large number of reviews indicate that a huge audience exists for this item and that it is in demand, which means that thousands of people are willing to spend money to get it. These analyses not only help you evaluate your competition but also enable you to understand what the public really desires. For example, if you search for duffel bags, reading through the reviews section will highlight areas where the product was not able to satisfy the customer; it might not have enough room or pockets, might not be water-proof, and suitable for camping trips, etc. This will facilitate you while you're designing your own duffel bag as you will be able to incorporate these in-demand features that other similar products lacked.

- Scroll through social media to find out the latest trends and what people are talking about

An excellent way to keep up with the latest trends is to use social media and determine what grabs your audience's attention. Focus on finding out issues, topics, and products that people are fascinated in and might want to purchase; you can do this by subscribing to people, pages, groups, and businesses that are related to your business idea. In this way, you can also observe and learn from their interactions with the target audience. All the knowledge that you could possibly need before beginning your venture is just one click away; use this to your advantage and let the voice of the people help you in manifesting your wildest dreams.

Still Got Too Many Passions? Try The 2-week Mini-project Technique To Narrow Down Your Passions

If you've somehow still ended up with multiple passions on your list, then the best way to weed out the non-essentials is to try them all out, one by one, in a two-week mini-project activity.

Sometimes, relying solely on your mind for answers can lead to a downward spiral of overthinking. Instead of supplying you with any answers, it simply continues to raise more questions until you're crippled with indecision and doubt. If you're the kind of person who can only achieve clarity through action, then this approach is highly recommended as it enables you to learn through a small-scale trial and error experiment. Think of yourself as a scientist who has to prove the existence of a particular phenomenon; suppose that your equations and calculations aren't enough to give you the answers that you need, so you set up an experiment to observe the results. This exercise will take time and energy, but it is bound to provide you with the solution to your passion problem. It is divided into four steps that you should follow over a span of two weeks to figure out whether a project is really your life's calling or just an activity, best reserved for the weekend.

1. Make a list of three things that you have a deep interest in and think of as your passions.

It might sound difficult for those of you who are struggling with more than three passions, but the idea is to keep your list small in order to prevent your mind from getting overwhelmed.

It might sound something like this: *'I'm interested in psychology because it's a fascinating field of study, and I'm always eager to learn about the workings of mind and behavior. I have dreamed about running my own clothing business ever since I was young, and the prospect really excites me. I also care about climate change and would like to see more fashion brands adopting environment-friendly business models and implementing policies to reduce waste, emissions, and the use of non-renewable energy sources.'*

So far, you have three ideas to choose from: psychology, business, and sustainable fashion.

2. Choose one option from the list you just created and dedicate yourself to learning all about it over two weeks.

In case you're suffering from another wave of FOBO, just pick the first one you wrote down: in this case, it's psychology.

3. Start with the smallest, easiest step.

Don't burn yourself out by diving down the deep end. If you picked psychology, start by searching for a book or course designed to familiarize beginners with the main concepts that define the field. You don't have to begin reading the book immediately. Take your time and start with a single Google search.

4. Build your way up to the finish line.

If you began your two-week challenge by searching for a good introductory book, then try reading the first chapter on the next day. Or watch the first fifteen minutes of a crash course video. Gradually make your way up to more challenging activities and observe your body's reaction to this exercise. Do you look forward to starting your day with a psychology-related activity? Does the subject truly nourish your curiosity and intellect? Or does it feel like another boring obligation that you have to fulfill for someone else's sake? How would you feel about interacting with experts in the field?

If you feel like you can't picture yourself pursuing this project at the end of these two weeks, then move on to the next item on your list. The objective is to repeat this exercise until you've found the thing that motivates you to get out of bed every morning and take on the entire world!

Chapter 8

The Law Of Attraction: How To Use It to Conquer All Hurdles

We've come a long way in our journey!

By this point, you might have realized what your one true passion is, which means that it is time to take the next step.

Do you know that everything about your body and mind can be reduced to a single, indestructible force that rules this entire universe?

Think beyond organs, cells, and neurons. When you find your passion, your heart and soul unite with nature to bring about external and internal harmony. However, this connection can only be achieved if you really push yourself to become sensitive to the world around you.

In this heightened state of awareness, you begin to realize that everything, from your body to the thoughts in your head, is made up of *energy*, pure and dynamic in its essence.

The Law of Attraction first gained popularity as a philosophical ideology of a nineteenth-century, healing campaign known as the New Thought Movement. So, what is this mysterious concept that worked for thousands of people, regardless of age, race, culture, and identity?

Like gravity, the Law of Attraction is fairly easy to grasp: its main principle dictates that everything in this universe tends to gravitate towards similar things. So like attracts like. The energy your thoughts, feelings, and behaviors emanate, whether or positive or negative, is going to influence what you get back from the universe. If you're a positive, optimistic person who is grateful and focused on inner peace, you're likely to attract good health, love, and other positive experiences that exist in the world.

We all firmly believe in the existence of physical laws. Let's take gravity as an example. It wasn't that gravity didn't exist until Newton's happy accident with the apple, it had been present since time immemorial; we just didn't know how to utilize it to our advantage simply because we were unaware of its reality.

This means that the key to a better, happier life has always been present inside of you. You can make your wildest dreams a reality if you open yourself up to a more positive, healthy approach to life. It doesn't matter if you believe in this law or not; it will continue to exist and impact your life; however, the sooner you begin to use it to attain the blissful, bountiful life that you've desired, the easier your journey to passion and fulfillment will appear.

You have the power to change your fate and emerge victorious from the cocoon of ignorance that has held you back your entire life. Why not give it a shot?

The formula needed to put this law to use is much easier to understand than the one used to explain gravity.

Now that you've decided on what goals, values, and passions you want to pursue in your life, your task is to let these positive, focused thoughts flow out into the universe.

To accomplish that, all you need to do is work towards your vision, have faith in your ability to get to the finish line, and remain open to feedback that you receive from yourself and the world.

When you refine your energy and turn it into a force that the universe will be glad to assimilate, it will begin to reciprocate in ways that you never dreamed were possible.

The 7 Laws Of Attraction

Let's take a look at the seven laws that make up this universal phenomenon and see how each one allows you to understand the purpose of making changes in your current lifestyle to make space for freedom, happiness, and warmth.

- Desire

Your heart and mind should be in total sync and filled with desire for what you want in life. The universe only responds to strong, positive emotion that lights up your entire being; unless you let go of the negative forces ruling your mind and shift your focus to healing, peace, and passion, you will continue to exist in a meaningless, lost state.

- Conceptualization and Imagination

The human mind has the astonishing power to create vivid images. This law requires that you take your day-dreaming one step further and visualize your goals until you begin to staunchly believe in their existence. Maybe your goal is to buy a house or a car. Think about it in as much detail as possible; use your imagination to conceptualize a complete image of what your ideal home would look like. Now picture yourself in your new, beautiful home and continue to refine the image by adding as many real, evocative details as possible.

- Affirmation

Positive affirmations can go a long way in strengthening our sense of self and solidifying our belief in what we want to achieve. The act of affirming is easy to practice in everyday life; just convince yourself through the power of positive words that what you want is already in existence and coming your way. These proclamations can even be about reminding yourself of what you already have in life and how it can help you achieve what you really, *really* want. Adding these affirmations to your daily routine can counteract the poisonous influence of self-defeating words and build up your resilience.

- Focus with Confidence

Concentrate on your goals until you cannot be distracted by the drama, negativity, and pessimism that permeates your environment. Your only task is to keep your head up and focus, and remain confident in the fact that whatever you desire will be given to you by the universe.

- Profound Belief

This goes beyond just having faith in your dreams or thinking that your goals will become a reality one day. You need to believe that whatever you desire is already a part of your life and has been manifested. Only through this resolve, strength, and conviction will you be able to experience the positivity that the universe sends your way.

- Gratitude

Ungratefulness can cause you to lose sight of the things that you already possess. It doesn't motivate you to do better; instead, you find yourself sinking down into self-pity and loathing; in short, your attitude breeds negativity and invites further depressing experiences into your life. Being grateful can change the way you perceive and interpret the world; start your day by giving thanks to the universe for being so kind to you, and you will immediately notice how it prepares you to take on challenges and make room for positivity and abundance.

- Manifestation

This marks the realization of your desire. Whatever you wanted from the universe has been given to you because you allowed yourself to open up to the blessings sent your way. All it took was changing the way you talk to yourself and talk about your passion to reflect that you're ready to deal with whatever comes in the way of you and your desire.

You might be wondering if there's anyone who can attest to the efficacy of this law.

If so, you'll be surprised at the sheer number of people who actively support, practice, and endorse this principle!

So what makes some people stand out from the crowd? Is it because they possess some innate qualities that other people don't, or is it because they're more receptive to positive forces and tend to migrate towards things that radiate similar energy?

Successful individuals such as Will Smith, Oprah Winfrey, Denzel Washington, Jim Carrey, Steve Harvey, Arnold Schwarzenegger, and Tyler Perry have testified to miraculous transformations in their lives once they began to comprehend and use the Law of Attraction to achieve the fame, wealth, and prosperity that they had only dared to dream of. Let's take a closer look at two celebrities who have extensively talked about the influence of this law on their lives and careers.

Celebrities Who Have Used The Law Of Attraction

- Will Smith

As an actor, a rapper, and a producer, Will Smith has gained an astonishing number of accolades throughout his prolific career; not only has he received four Grammy Awards, but also he has been nominated for two Academy Awards and five Golden Globe Awards for his achievements in music and film. A firm believer in the Law of Attraction, Smith has often talked about how negativity stems from a lack of control over our thoughts. Research studies have shown that on a daily basis, the average human has around 50,000 thoughts, out of which 70% are negative. He claims that it's impossible to succeed unless you begin by controlling what you let in and out of your own mind. Since thoughts precede reality, it's important that we declutter our minds to give space to positive affirmations and self-love; what we put out into this world, whether it be negative emotions, thoughts, or behaviors, comes back to us like a boomerang. "Our thoughts, our feelings, our dreams, our ideas are physical in the universe." Smith asserts. "That if we dream something, if we picture something, it adds a physical thrust towards the realization that we can put into the Universe" (Leonard, 2018).

He emphasizes the importance of creating a new, uplifting reality for yourself by using the mind's astonishing powers of visualization in order to push back the negativity and despair that often chips away at our passion. "I believe that I can create whatever I want to create." Smith declares, highlighting the significance of unwavering desire and imagination. "If I can put my head on it right, study it, learn the patterns, and — it's hard to put into words, it's real metaphysical, esoteric nonsense, but I feel very strongly that we are who we choose to be" (Leonard, 2018).

- Arnold Schwarzenegger

In the 1970s, the actor, body-builder, politician, and businessman was interviewed by sports-writer Steve Chandler, who worked at the Tucson Citizen. Schwarzenegger had yet to achieve fame for his incredible contributions to the film industry and was only able to get roles in negatively-reviewed films that did not manage to grasp the attention of the audience. However, when Chandler asked him about the next project he was going to take up after body-building,

Schwarzenegger calmly replied that "I am going to be the number-one box-office star in all of Hollywood."

Chandler was bewildered at his confidence and taken aback by his staunch belief in the statement. When he asked Schwarzenegger to talk about how he would manage to achieve such a feat, he shared his recipe to success. "It's the same process I used in bodybuilding," Arnold clarified. "What you do is create a vision of who you want to be, and then live into that picture as if it were already true."

And soon enough, Schwarzenegger was able to realize his dreams of becoming a box-office hit with the release of his widely acclaimed *Terminator* movies. Later on, he was able to manifest his vision of becoming a politician and businessman by applying the same formula: conceptualizing his deepest desires and trusting the mind and the universe to come together to help him attain his ambitions.

You might be thinking that it all sounds too good to be true. If the world worked on this principle, everyone would be infinitely happier and more at peace than they are now.

Yes, they would.

The reason why you don't see more satisfied and fulfilled adults around you is that they don't believe in the Law of Attraction; they become skeptical and cynical, refusing to trust their mind and heart, dismissing this phenomenon simply because they cannot see it.

However, just because you can't see something, doesn't mean that it isn't real.

If it worked for other people, it should work for you! After all, it only demands that you firmly believe in the possibility of happiness and growth. What could possibly go wrong?

Ways To Use The Law Of Attraction Every Day

So let's begin by discussing seven strategies that you can incorporate in your daily routine, which will alter your outlook on life forever. If used properly and consistently, these techniques will begin to yield immediate results; you will feel lighter, more optimistic, and ready to tackle any challenges that the world throws at you.

Excited? Let's start with the smallest steps that you can take today!

- The bathroom post-it trick

Never forget that your thoughts have the strength to alter reality and influence your environment. Everything begins with a single, positive thought; unless you replace the toxicity with optimism and happiness, you will remain stuck in an inactive, stagnant state. Positive thought gives rise to vital energy, which influences even the smallest of our actions. These actions send energy out into the universe, like radio signals. For the world to respond to your faith, gratitude, and optimism, it is important that your thoughts and behaviors reflect your desire and conviction to manifest your dreams.

To do this, take a post-it note or any plain card, write down a sentence that reminds you of how your current thoughts are going to help you create a better, brighter future and put it against your bathroom mirror. In this way, you will be constantly surrounded by reminders to put your trust in the power of your thoughts.

Example: *My positive thoughts are creating a happy and wealthy life for me.*

- Think and speak positively

Remember how we talked about the significance of positive affirmations earlier on in this chapter? The idea is to replace negative thought patterns and self-defeating beliefs that you have assimilated over time, with optimistic statements that remind you to be the best person you can be so that you are able to manifest positive experiences in your life.

These statements should always be in present-tense. This is because you want to be kind to yourself and talk in an upbeat manner as if you have managed to accomplish all your desired goals and are currently living your best life.

An example of this would be to say: *'I am incredibly grateful and overjoyed that I have X and find myself satisfied at the end of every day because I'm pursuing my passion.'*

Replace X with your desire, and remember to keep on repeating this to yourself throughout the day. This will prevent your focus from wavering and help you keep your eyes on the goal, no matter what happens.

- Gratitude journal

It might seem hard to concentrate on the good things in life when you're low. You might feel like there's nothing that could possibly bring you joy and so you keep sinking deeper and deeper into negativity. A gratitude journal can prevent this from happening! All you have to do is catalog your favorite things about life, every day and talk about why they make you feel blessed. In this way, whenever you feel hopeless and sad, you can always flip through this journal and recount your blessings. It can be simple appreciations of the weather, your food, your healthy body, your friends, partners, etc. You will experience an immediate shift from despair to gratitude, which will improve your mood, boost your morale, and put you in an optimistic state of mind.

- To-do lists

To-do lists are extremely helpful in a lot of ways. They allow you to set clear daily goals for yourself, help you in prioritizing all your tasks, declutter your mind, and act as a reminder of everything that needs to be done. This clarity gives way to determination and concentration. And besides, isn't it extremely satisfying when you can cross items off your list?

- Set goals using the law of attraction

When you begin to use the principles mentioned above to set your goals, you will begin to notice an increase in your productivity, concentration, and motivation. This is because prior to acquiring this knowledge about the law of attraction, your goals were only abstractions and incomplete ideas in your mind. Two important aspects when setting your goals using the law of attraction are clarity and positivity. Make sure to clarify your goals as much as possible. Let's say if you want a perfect partner. How tall is he/she? What color is his/her hair? What hobbies does he/she have? Make sure your goals are positive and bring you positive feelings when you think about them.

- Repeat, Repeat, Repeat

This isn't a quick, short-term fix for your problems.

The law of attraction won't work unless you stand by it every single day and implement the aforementioned strategies. Repeat each exercise until you're able to achieve the desired results. Remember, repetition is key! Now that you're finally setting out on this wondrous journey, your job is to commit to your dreams until you're able to manifest them!

Chapter 9

Convert Your Passion Into A Profession

So far, we've talked at length about different topics that revolve around finding your passion and becoming a more productive, healthy person.

Now, it's time for action.

This chapter is dedicated entirely to practical strategies, key points, and questions that will form the foundation of your master plan, essential for turning your passion into a profitable venture.

But before we can move on to these defining questions, let's recap what we already know about passion.

Differentiating Between A Hobby And A Profitable Passion

As we've discussed before, a hobby is not the same as a passion; it's easy to confuse the two, but when you force yourself to treat your hobby as a profitable passion, you just run into yet another dead-end. Being interested in and skilled at something doesn't mean that it's your passion! There is another risk involved in such a scheme; when you turn your hobby to a profitable profession, a tremendous shift occurs in your cognition. This changes your relationship with your hobby from *'I love doing (X)'* to *'I have to do (X)'*. If your hobby starts to feel like a chore, abort your mission! This is your heart's way of telling you to keep searching for your passion. Only once you're certain about your decision should you proceed to the next step: figuring out the four different angles that you can use to turn your passion into a profitable profession.

- Different angles you can use to make your passion into a profitable profession
  - Technology

Do you have an idea about an app, website, machinery, or technology that could be useful to other professionals in your niche? Perhaps you can create a database that helps customers track their orders or an application that could benefit artists and designers. When the founder of Netflix first got the idea of it wanted to try if they can rent the DVD online instead of having to go to the DVD store, which people usually forget to return and end up paying a late fee. He was initially laughed at by everyone, but now he owns a company that has a net worth of over 100 billion dollars! Ask yourself whether you have an idea that could solve logistical problems for different businesses and then channel your energy into bringing this idea to reality!

- Talk

Are you a proficient public speaker, blogger, or writer? Do you love talking about things and creating content that spreads awareness about a particular topic or subject? If so, then this angle is perfect for you! It doesn't matter what you're passionate about; it can be topics like environment, mental health, fashion, travel, and much more—all you have to do is share your knowledge with the public. Create blogs, short films, documentaries, or write a book and provide online classes to educate people about your passion!

- Advice

If you're an expert in customizing certain aspects of your passion to fit other people, then this might be right up your alley! By becoming a consultant, you will be able to offer advice to your clients through one-on-one interactions; for example, if you're interested in fashion and think you have something to say, become a stylist!

- Community

This angle is perfect for sociable people, with interest in organizing events and meeting other individuals with the same passion! Let's continue with the previous example: as someone who loves the world of fashion, you could organize events and invite other aspiring fashion designers to present their work so that you can create a space for fellow professionals to meet and share their creativity.

- Questions To Ask

Time for another question and answer session to refine your profitable passion. Here are four things that you need to ask yourself before you start working on your project:

- Who can help you that's equally passionate?

Think about all the people in your life who can help you progress further and attain your goals. Who pushes you to do better and makes you view yourself in a positive light, even on days when you can't. Keeping these passionate individuals close can help you stay committed to your goal!

- What strengths do you have, and what will you need to outsource?

No matter how tempting it might be to do everything yourself, you need to be realistic and find out what skills, connections, and strengths you bring to the table. If you need additional help in evaluating yourself, use the Myers-Briggs personality test given in chapter 1 to find out your strengths and weaknesses. This will help you understand what needs to be outsourced to other people in order for your idea to work!

- What networks do you have, and what networks can you build?

Assessing your connections is a smart, meticulous method of figuring out how to get to the next level. This question will enable you to get help from the networks you have already established and understand what people, companies, and organizations need to be contacted in order for your business to flourish. Let's say you want to work in an investment bank, but you don't know who to talk to. Finding an internship in a bank or a company that works with investment banks will help you build your networks that way.

- Is it worth doing it for free?

Test the waters before jumping into the deep end!

Try doing it for free for a month; if your idea was to become a stylist, take a small step in that direction by styling a few close friends or relatives and see whether you actually enjoy the task. If it's worth doing for free and gives you that deep contentment and happiness that you were looking for, then voila! You've hit the jackpot!

Now it's time that we jump right into the three strategies that can turn your passion project into reality.

3 Steps To Getting Your Project Underway

- How to set goals: Follow the 'breadcrumbs' approach

How many times have you abandoned an idea because you tried to do everything all at once?

You felt that zing of energy and tried to get you rolling, but only to leave the project unfinished because you realized half-way through that it wasn't working out.

Rome wasn't built in a day, so what makes you think that you can figure out all the details in no time at all?

To create anything worthwhile, you have to follow the 'breadcrumbs' approach. Start with the smallest step and keep repeating it until you have enough energy to advance to the next level. When you start setting daily goals, remind yourself that you're human, prone to exhaustion, and easily overwhelmed when you have too much to do. Live by the second and think of your passion project as a building; you can't make a skyscraper in a week! It might take days, but the result will be worth every single brick that you put in place.

- o Set budgets

Start by setting a budget for your project. Assess your financial condition and the risks associated with starting this venture. Spend considerable time deciding how to allocate your money to different resources.

- o Set dates

Then progress to the next step: setting up your schedule for a month. Try to plan your days and make sure you take social and professional commitments into account. This allows you to predict and plan how to spend your time so that you can focus on what needs to be done and when!

- Build expertise

Don't set unrealistic expectations for yourself—that way lies danger and disappointment. If you expect yourself to be perfect from day one, you will only be disillusioned by the reality. The truth is that no one becomes a master in an instant, you have to build up your expertise by all means available; take online classes, crash courses, read articles and books, and listen to experts in your field—just make sure that you give yourself enough time to accumulate the knowledge that you need to attain your goals!

- How to analyze your competition

Unless you analyze your competition, you'll never be able to set yourself apart from the crowd and make people realize that your services are better suited to their needs. Study your competitors to find out how you can improve the quality of your service and product; investigate the general reaction and reviews left by the customers. Can you offer something that these companies cannot? Can you eliminate the complaints of the customers by launching a better product?

In essence, your plan should cover all aspects so that you are clear about your values, purpose, goal, and execution.

- Journal Exercise: 5-year plan

Get your journals out again! We're planning our future!

On a new page, draw five rows and two columns. Each row should have a specific timeframe; I prefer to start from 5 years and narrow it down to 1 hour. Now label the two columns as 'personal' and 'professional'. Your task is to list your goals for each heading until you begin to get an idea about your current situation and your ultimate goal. The idea is to create a holistic plan and then narrow down your focus until you begin to understand your priorities. Commit to one goal from each row and try to accomplish it within the specified time frame. Even though you'll be tempted to revise these goals, resist and keep working! It will be something like the following table.

5 years	Make one million dollars profit by selling products through E-commerce.
4 months	Make a revenue of 5k dollars by selling products through E-commerce.
3 weeks	Got a website that promotes all the products you are selling.
2 days	Set up your websites and find the products you want to sell.
1 hour	Find online courses to learn about the E-commerce businesses you can do.

- The 30 before 7:30 rule

Popularized by Mel Robbins, this strategy allows you to plan your day before you actually get out of bed. Robbins recommends not looking at your phone right before you go to sleep, and right after you wake up, this allows your mind to take a break from the constant flow of information and actually focus on what needs to get done throughout the day.

Two Paths Through Which You Can Pursue Your Passion

Now let's talk about what you need to be doing so that you don't become a person who cannot keep up with paying the bills and putting food on the table for the family or yourself when pursuing your passion.

From here onwards, you can choose one of two paths; you can either find your passion through your job or pursue your passion on the side. In order to find out which one works best for you, take a look at the advantages and disadvantages that accompany each route.

- Path 1: Finding your passion through your job

One way to find your passion is to continue at your current job and slowly progress until you're able to eliminate the parts of your job that you don't like and expand those that excite and challenge you. This is a low-risk approach that is perfect for those who are certain about what they want to do and the profitability of their profession. For example, you can search for job openings within the company you are currently working at and see if there is a job opening that is perfect for you. Let's say if you want to pursue a career in finance but currently working in the HR department; you can see if your company is seeking a financial specialist. Usually, companies are more likely to hire their own employees for these positions since they know them well, and there is less risk associated with re-positioning an existing employee than hiring a new employee. However, an obvious disadvantage is that progress is almost always gradual, and by the time you get to a position where you can control what you want to do and how, you might regret your entire decision. It is also based on probability since you can never be sure that you'll be able to achieve such a position.

- Path 2: Find your passion as a side job

The other path is less common and more dangerous. It exists in various forms: you can work at a job that does not satisfy you and either pursue your passion on the side or hold off on doing what you love until you save up enough money and resources to pursue your goals full-time. This is ideal for people who have passions that are in direct contradiction to their day job. For example, if you work in finance but would love to become a singer, this approach gives you the freedom to pay your expenses while still staying in touch with your desires, instead of waiting around to get a promotion. However, if you continue to pay the bills by working at your day job, there's a high chance that you will get sucked into its tedium and lose the creativity that drives your passion.

It all relies on your personality and preference; the key is to not make a final decision unless you have a solid understanding of who you are and what you want. Don't let ignorance and youth dictate your life. A fact about a person who knows his purpose in life: He never gives in. Wait a minute; it is not because he has never been knocked down, rather his ability to not accept defeat, no matter what hardships lie ahead. How can you surrender when a fire, as strong as ever, is igniting inside you?

It will be really appreciated if you could take just 60 seconds to write a brief review on Amazon, even if it's just a few sentences!

Conclusion

D id you find what you were looking for? That missing puzzle piece in the jigsaw of life?

The objective of this book was to provide a multidimensional approach to finding your passion and purpose in life. It isn't just any self-help book, filled with motivational quotes and inspiring stories; instead, it provides you with a meticulous approach featuring hundreds of different strategies, recommended by experts, which have been specially designed to help you explore your full potential in life. While the focus of this book was to help you get closer to your passion, it also contains discussions on all topics relevant to personal and professional development: from teaching you to set boundaries and say no to detailed discussions on fear, failure, distractions, and the advantages of listening to your heart—this book covers a broad set of skills and tools you need to take on the world. Not only does it help you understand what you want but also enables you to explore *who* you are so that you can create a plan that reflects your unique approach, style, and talents.

However, the scope of this book is not limited to practical strategies; while it helps you differentiate between passion and hobbies, enables you to refine your passion project until it is profitable, and provides you with a complete plan on how to adopt a balanced lifestyle, it also discusses the usefulness of those more abstract concepts that are often undermined despite their efficacy such as the law of attraction, meditation, positive affirmations, and profound belief.

Remember, you hold the keys within you to breakthrough.

The critical part is to expel those limitations so that you can advance your life to the next level. Let the person you want to be, breaks through the wall of mediocrity that wants you to stay as who you are, and see the successful self-made entrepreneur that you want to become. That individual, that vision, and that dream that you carry within yourself are the things that can set you free. Explore the themes of redemption, about hope, about renewal in this book. Every soul can dream, and each moment is created to bring us closer to that transformative journey.

It is about finding that moment when everything stops and suddenly looks different.

It is about finding your own awakening.

So take all of this energy, knowledge, and insight that you've gained over the last few days, step out of your comfort zone and become a better, truer, and freer version of yourself.

Your Success Booklet
(Don't forget to grab this!)

This booklet includes:

- ➢ 9 things that successful people are different from the mediocre
- ➢ 15 things successful people say no to
- ➢ 8 Steps to achieve anything you want in life

Get yourself mentally equipped before the journey starts.
To receive your success booklet, visit the link:

https://beausuccess.activehosted.com/f/1

Resources

49 Ways To Say No To Anyone (When You Don't Want To Be A Jerk). (2019, October 9). Career FAQs. https://www.careerfaqs.com.au/news/news-and-views/how-to-say-no-to-anyone

Ayres, V. (2017, August 25). What It Means to Just Be Yourself and 3 Ways to Do It. Tiny Buddha. https://tinybuddha.com/blog/what-it-means-to-just-be-yourself-and-how-to-do-it/

Baulch, J. (2019, May 1). Self-Awareness: The Key to Taking Care of Your Mental Health and Wellbeing. Inner Melbourne Clinical Psychology. https://www.innermelbpsychology.com.au/self-awareness-mental-health/

Beaton, C. (2016, June 29). The Too-Many-Passions Problem: 4 Tips To Help Millennials Choose A Perfect Career. Forbes. https://www.forbes.com/sites/carolinebeaton/2016/03/29/the-too-many-passions-problem-4-things-you-can-do-today-to-choose-your-perfect-career/#3e8ae14c29af

Bennett, C. (2014, July 25). The Importance of Checking In With Yourself. Psychology Today. https://www.psychologytoday.com/us/blog/heartache-hope/201407/the-importance-checking-in-yourself

Canfield, J. (2020, July 21). Achieve Any Goal With the Law of Attraction. Jack Canfield. https://www.jackcanfield.com/blog/goal-setting-law-of-attraction/

Capritto, A. (2019, December 3). How to say no to things you don't want to do. CNET. https://www.cnet.com/health/how-to-say-no-to-things-you-dont-want-to-do/

Castrillon, C. (2020, April 24). 5 Steps To Turn Passion Into Profit. Forbes. https://www.forbes.com/sites/carolinecastrillon/2020/03/08/5-steps-to-turn-passion-into-profit/#2aded06d700b

Copadis, A. (2020, February 12). 11 Steps to Choosing Your Most Profitable Niche. Income School. https://incomeschool.com/11-steps-choosing-profitable-niche/

Davenport, B. (2020, July 4). 50 Self-Coaching Questions To Help You Find Your Passion. Live Bold and Bloom. https://liveboldandbloom.com/02/passion-in-life/questions-to-find-life-passion

Dowches-Wheeler, J. (2018, February 20). 7 Questions to Ask to Discover Your Passion. Jessica DW | Spiritual Leadership Coach. https://jessicadw.com/blog/find-your-passion

Duczeminski, M. (2015, March 26). 10 Reasons Why People Who Read A Lot Are More Likely To Be Successful. Lifehack. https://www.lifehack.org/articles/communication/10-reasons-people-read-lot-likely-successful.html#:%7E:text=They%20have%20increased%20focus,isn%27t%20a%20quick%20process.&text=Readers%20take%20breaks%2C%20naturally%2C%20but,they%27ve%20dove%20into%20it

Eby, D. (2020, July 2). 8 Ways to Turn Your Passion into Profits. The Inner Entrepreneur. http://theinnerentrepreneur.com/761/8-ways-to-turn-your-passion-into-profits/

Elizabeth, A. (2020a, March 12). How to Overcome Fear and Realize Your Potential (The Ultimate Guide). Lifehack. https://www.lifehack.org/articles/lifestyle/3-simple-steps-to-overcome-fear.html

Elizabeth, A. (2020b, March 12). How to Overcome Fear and Realize Your Potential (The Ultimate Guide). Lifehack. https://www.lifehack.org/articles/lifestyle/3-simple-steps-to-overcome-fear.html

Ferreira, N. M. (2020a, April 20). How to Be Successful (And Get Everything You Want in Life). Oberlo. https://www.oberlo.com/blog/how-to-be-successful

Ferreira, N. M. (2020b, April 29). How to Find Your Passion (And Live Your Best Life) - Oberlo. Oberlo. https://www.oberlo.com/blog/how-to-find-your-passion

Gordon-Barnes, C. (2020, June 19). 6 Fresh Ways to Find Your Passion. The Muse. https://www.themuse.com/advice/6-fresh-ways-to-find-your-passion

Graham, P. (2006, January). How to Do What You Love. Paul Graham. http://www.paulgraham.com/love.html

Harris, R., & PhD, H. S. (2011). The Confidence Gap: A Guide to Overcoming Fear and Self-Doubt (1st ed.). Trumpeter.

Ho, L. (2020, April 6). How To Make A Vision Board That Works. Lifehack. https://www.lifehack.org/292677/how-creating-vision-board-will-empower-you-manifest-your-dream-life

How to Choose a Career When You Have Many Passions. (2019, September 25). Work You Love Coach. https://www.workyoulovecoach.com/how-to-pick-a-focus-when-you-have-many-passions

How to look after your mental health. (2020, April 30). Mental Health Foundation. https://www.mentalhealth.org.uk/publications/how-to-mental-health

How to overcome fear and anxiety. (2020, April 30). Mental Health Foundation. https://www.mentalhealth.org.uk/publications/overcome-fear-anxiety

How to Overcome Your Fears, Get Unstuck, and Fuel Your Success |... (2019, October 17). Brian Tracy's Self Improvement & Professional Development Blog. https://www.briantracy.com/blog/personal-success/fight-or-flight-overcoming-your-fears/

Hurst, K. (2016, January 13). Use The Law Of Attraction To Set Goals The Right Way. The Law Of Attraction. https://www.thelawofattraction.com/use-law-of-attraction-to-set-goals-right/

Jackson, N. M. (2012, March 6). Six Tips to Turn Your Passion into Profit. Entrepreneur. https://www.entrepreneur.com/article/222971

Herrera, T. (2018, July 30). How to Beat F.O.B.O., From the Expert Who Coined It.. https://www.nytimes.com/2018/07/30/smarter-living/how-to-beat-fobo-from-the-expert-who-coined-it.html

Khan, C. (2019, November 24). Do you take hours to make a simple decision? You may have Fobo. The Guardian. https://www.theguardian.com/global/2019/nov/24/fear-of-missing-out-fomo-making-decision-biology-fobo-christmas-turkey

Leonard, M. (2018, August 16). 4 Thought Provoking Will Smith Quotes on the Law of Attraction. Fearless Soul - Inspirational Music & Life Changing Thoughts. https://iamfearlesssoul.com/will-smith-quotes-law-attraction/

Lounge, T. (2019, June 25). Seven Steps To Using the Law of Attraction to Manifest Your Dreams. Thrive Lounge. http://www.thriveloungedc.com/blog/seven-steps-law-of-attraction-manifest-dreams

Manson, M. (2020, June 8). 7 Strange Questions That Help You Find Your Life... Mark Manson. https://markmanson.net/life-purpose

Maros, M. (2016, October 31). Checking In With Yourself. Peaceful Mind Peaceful Life. https://peacefulmindpeacefullife.org/checking-in-with-yourself/

McFadden, C. (2020, July 20). Turn Your Passion into Profit with These 7 Helpful Tips for Building a Hobby-Based Business. Interesting Engineering. https://interestingengineering.com/turn-your-passion-into-profit-with-these-7-helpful-tips-for-building-a-hobby-based-business

mindbodygreen. (2020, February 26). 7 Scientific Reasons You Should Listen To Your Heart (Not Your Brain). https://www.mindbodygreen.com/0-11982/7-scientific-reasons-you-should-listen-to-your-heart-not-your-brain.html#:%7E:text=The%20heart%20emits%20more%20electrical,stronger%20that%20of%20the%20brain.

Naidoo, U. (2019, August 29). Nutritional strategies to ease anxiety. Harvard Health Blog. https://www.health.harvard.edu/blog/nutritional-strategies-to-ease-anxiety-201604139441

Patel, D. (2018, December 12). 7 Proven Strategies for Overcoming Distractions. Entrepreneur. https://www.entrepreneur.com/article/324560

Payne, K. (2020, April 26). The Beginner's Guide To Turn Your Passion Into Profits. Kevintpayne.Com. https://kevintpayne.com/turn-passion-into-profits/

Rampton, J. (2017, November 20). A 5-Step Formula To Find Your Niche. Forbes. https://www.forbes.com/sites/johnrampton/2017/11/07/a-5-step-formula-to-find-your-niche/#4d4ab93a48fc

Rytarowska, S. (2014, February 20). 10 Ways To Remove The Distractions That Keep You From Doing the Best At Work. Lifehack. https://www.lifehack.org/articles/productivity/10-ways-remove-the-distractions-that-keep-you-from-doing-the-best-work.html

Sandford, K. (2020a, May 12). 10 Things You Can Do Now to Change Your Life Forever. Lifehack. https://www.lifehack.org/310325/10-things-change-your-life-forever

Sandford, K. (2020b, May 12). 10 Things You Can Do Now to Change Your Life Forever. Lifehack. https://www.lifehack.org/310325/10-things-change-your-life-forever

Sommer, E. (2017, September 24). 5 Toxic Distractions That Stop You Getting What You Want. Live Purposefully Now. https://livepurposefullynow.com/toxic-distractions-getting-in-your-way/

Steimle, J. (2016, January 12). 14 Ways To Conquer Fear. Forbes. https://www.forbes.com/sites/joshsteimle/2016/01/04/14-ways-to-conquer-fear/#1d1b72ba1c48

Stiefvater, S. (2019, July 8). How to Use the Law of Attraction to Achieve Your Goals (or at Least Become a More Positive Person). PureWow. https://www.purewow.com/wellness/how-to-use-the-law-of-attraction

Timus, C. (2019, November 12). 10 Celebrities who Love the Law of Attraction. Apply the Law of Attraction. https://www.applythelawofattraction.com/celebrities-law-attraction/

Turner, A. (2019, October 4). 6 Journal Prompts To Get Clear On What You Really Want. Medium. https://medium.com/@alexturner_5843/6-journal-prompts-to-get-clear-on-what-you-really-want-ec45d27488d6

Verma, P. (2019, September 6). "I Don't Know What My Passion Is" — The Perfect Solution. Medium. https://medium.com/the-mission/how-to-find-your-true-passion-and-live-a-life-you-wont-regret-on-your-deathbed-c58ce450beaf

Vozza, S. (2016, February 17). The Ultimate Guide To Saying No To Things You Don't Want To Do. Fast Company. https://www.fastcompany.com/3056562/the-ultimate-guide-to-saying-no-to-things-you-dont-want-to

Wang, S. Y. (2020, July 14). Tired Of Trying To "Figure Out" What You Really Want To Do? Try This Instead. Forbes. https://www.forbes.com/sites/sarayoungwang/2018/03/26/tired-of-trying-to-figure-out-what-you-really-want-to-do-try-this-instead/#31c466802f9b

Wiest, B. (2018, September 21). 22 Microhabits That Will Completely Change Your Life In A Year. Forbes. https://www.forbes.com/sites/briannawiest/2018/09/18/22-microhabits-that-will-completely-change-your-life-in-2-years/#7468256c1035

Willis, J. (2011, July 12). The Brain-Based Benefits of Writing for Math and Science Learning. Edutopia. https://www.edutopia.org/blog/writing-executive-function-brain-research-judy-willis

Winfield, C. (2020, June 30). How to Make a Daily Routine to Become Your Best Self. Buffer Resources. https://buffer.com/resources/daily-success-routine/

www.ingramcontent.com/pod-product-compliance
Lightning Source LLC
Chambersburg PA
CBHW020910080526
44589CB00011B/527